Contents:
1. Introduction.
2. The Concept of Strategic Human Resource Management.
2.1. Definitions.
2.1.1. Strategy.
2.1.2. Human Resource.
2.1.3. Strategic Human Resource Management (SHRM).
2.2. Points of View in SHRM.
2.2.1. Best Fit.
2.2.2. Best Practice.
2.2.3. Perspective of the company according to the resources.
3. The Idea of Sustainability in HRM.
3.1. Definitions.
3.1.1. Sustainability.
3.1.2. Management of a sustainable form of resources.
3.1.3. Sustainable HRM.
3.2. Approaches in Sustainable HRM.
3.2.1. Capability Reproduction.
3.2.2. Promoting Social and Environmental Health.
3.2.3. Connections.
4. Differences & Commonalities.
4.1. A Shift of Paradigm.
4.2. The Heart of the Matter.
4.3. The Connection between Sustainability and SHRM.
4.4. From Strategic HRM to Sustainable HRM: a new approach?
5. Case Study: The Bremer Landesbank and Sustainable HRM.
6. Conclusion & Discussion.
References.
Online resources.

1. Introduction.

The world we live in today, is constantly changing and anticipating events and predicting how they unfold in an ambiguous and complex environment has become more challenging than ever before. These circumstances are generally known as a VUCA world, a medium that is peculiarized by instability, doubt, diversity and indetermination.

Under these circumstances leading and managing businesses, has become a major challenge especially with regard to political and social pressure that lies upon the CEOs of the different organizations. In this context, the term sustainability, has become some kind of a buzzword, and shifted into the focus of attention in the last years. Although the topic as such is not new, the sustainability debate is experiencing new impulses from different fields and perspectives.

Wherever we go, wherever we look, in some ways we will always be confronted with different facets of sustainability. Especially, due to the omnipresent debate on global warming and climate change, we cannot fail to delve into this topic a little more.

Fifteen years after the Kyoto Protocol, which extends the United Nations Framework Convention on Climate Change, and which represents the first binding contract under international law concerning greenhouse gases, the necessity to establish legal frameworks for organizations with regard to a sustainable and responsible handling of natural resources, in particular with the Fridays For Future demonstrations in mind, becomes more than apparent.

Presumably, it will take a couple of years until the laws and regulations are fully implemented, but for the sake of the environment it is good to know that, a lot of organizations, already engage very closely with this topic and that the debate on sustainability has also arrived in the realm of management.

This book focuses on the topic of sustainability in the realm of human resource management. People management, or human resource management, belongs to the younger disciplines of management; however, early beginnings can be traced back to 1878, when in the US the 60-hour working week for women and children was regulated by law. What seems to make us shudder nowadays, was one of the first milestones in human resource management, because it underlined the necessity of taking needs of employees seriously to prevent a radicalization of the situation.

At the turn of the century, first personnel offices were established, however, they were more occupied with administration and accounting. The First World War then, can be seen as a decisive event in people management as old and entrenched patterns of thought were left behind, as for example unions were accepted by politics; and finally, the 8-hour working day was introduced. Also, the global economic crisis and the Second World War, ignited the discussion about modern working conditions.

In the 1950's, when the economy was booming, and workforce was scarce organizations, started appreciating the workforce and a humanization of work was discussed and received new inputs in the 1970's, when new methods of personnel development, such as coaching and mentoring, made its way from the US to Europe.

Over the last decades, employees were treated more respectfully and as a precious resource, the working world became more flexible and new options, such as working from home were made possible. In particular, non-monetary key figures, like satisfaction and commitment became important indicators for the management. Thus, the evolvement from a mere administrative function of personnel management, to a Strategic Human Resource Management (SHRM) becomes apparent.

The question that arises now is, when the question of sustainability is joined with the question of sustainable management of human resources, how can we define sustainable management of human resources? Where are the similarities and antagonistic points with respect to SHRM? Is it an alternative point of view or is it really a paradigm shift?

Research that addresses the issue of sustainability is still very premature, as this area of research is only an emerging one. On the other hand, we can already count on a small number of experts on the subject, who have already contributed interesting theories on the subject. If we focus on the German research community, Müller-Christ studies, can find the first beginnings dealing with the idea of sustainability in HRM. Even more relevant concerning the conceptualization is Ehnert, who is more or less the originator of this field. But, also in the international research community contributions can be found, for instance, by Kramar and Mariappanadar .

Regarding the topic of SHRM, a plethora of literature can be found, since this field of research has already emerged in the 1980's. Well known writers are for instance Boxall, Wright, Huselid, Schuler & Jackson, to just mention a few.

In the first part of this book, strategic human resources management (SHRM) will be explored in greater depth. The concepts of strategy, human resources and human resources management will be explained, and the most successful models in the field of human resources management will be provided, with the aim of understanding how personnel management is currently applied.

The second part will deal with the notion of sustainability, and will present the different points of view in the field of sustainable management of human resources.

In the third part, both concepts will be contrasted with each other, and differences and commonalities will be presented in detail. The main purpose of this section of the book, is to answer the question of whether it is possible to contemplate a paradigm shift in the equation of the two concepts. Furthermore, the central difference between both approaches, will be displayed and its main aspects will be outlined. Apart from that, parallels of both approaches will be pointed out, and the question if an evolvement from SHRM to Sustainable HRM can be perceived will be tackled.

A case study on the Bremer Landesbank will demonstrate the successful implementation of theoretical Sustainable HRM frameworks into practice.

The last chapter will summarize the insights acquired in the preceding sections and will show some aspects that are worthwhile to examine more closely.

2. The Concept of Strategic Human Resource Management.

2.1. Definitions.

At first, before having a closer look at the approaches and concepts in SHRM, it is useful to establish some definitions of the key terms, in order to create a common understanding of the topic.

2.1.1 Strategy.

As for the term "strategy" or "strategic", there is no definition which is collectively accepted among researchers. The etymology of the word itself originates in the ancient Greek word strategos, which comes, in turn, from the two words stratos (army) and agein (to lead) and which we can translate into our language as to lead the military.
Apart from the military meaning and interpretation of the word strategy, it was also used in a business context to outline the conduct of companies. Staehle (1999), also states that the military, as well as the firm need to handle the situation of rare resources to implement their objectives, in order to be able to compete.
In management theory, the concept of strategy became more popular after it was introduced into the business policy courses at Harvard University in in the 1960s. Staehle (1999) also states that, both in the military and in the company field, in order to be able to implement the objectives necessary to be able to compete, it is necessary to control human resources.

In human resource management theory, the concept of strategy became popular when, in the 1960s, Harvard University introduced it, to its courses in corporate policy. One of the most widely used viewpoints in strategy research and practice today, is the so-called classical approach or rational planning approach, which is the most commonly used in management and research practice.

In this sense, the strategy is defined as a sequential link of individual decisions, with the aim of creating a harmonization or strategic reciprocity between the institution and its environment. It is proposed that the strategic adjustment be put into practice by locating the strengths and weaknesses of the organization, in order to take advantage of opportunities and, in turn, avoid threats within its business sector. Strategies are derived from corporate goals, and serve as an instrument to achieve a certain purpose.

Characteristics that are attributed to the term strategic, for instance, are relevance, simplification, and proactivity (Scholz, 1987), highlighting the emphasis of what is significant, the focus on key elements and the strive for acting in good time. Staehle (1999) also uses the term proactive as another word for planning. In this regard, strategic actions are durable, environment-oriented, systematic and holistic.

However, there is discussion that the understanding of the term strategy is not in a broader sense. First, because the correlation between corporate goals and strategies belongs to the most discussed issues in the field of strategy research. And second, the dynamic environment makes it impossible to strive for strategies with a long-standing planning horizon. Macharzina (2003), on the other hand, proposes to consider strategies as master plans to be applied in times of environmental change.

A more pluralistic view, has been proposed by Mintzberg et al. (2003), stating that strategy might have different appearances in reality. They offer five different interpretations of the strategy concept: a planning, a script, a strategy, a positioning and a perspective.

However, since not all envisioned strategies are implemented, Mintzberg suggests to distinguish between intended and realized strategies. Hence, as realized strategies are not always intended, they are located between deliberate and emergent strategies. Also, reality shows that, only in some cases plans, can be put into practice in the exact same way as originally intended. In fact, the implementation of the strategy includes quite a few surprise factors and, therefore, some of these strategies are not put into practice.

This knowledge of strategy admits the fact that strategy has different possible viewpoints in corporate application, and integrates the perception that strategies put into practice cannot be planned a priori in a rational and inflexible way.

For the purpose of this book, and the following explanations and remarks this understanding of strategy, is considered to be appropriate.

2.1.2 Human Resource.

In a generic sense, the term resource can be understood as:

"a stock or supply of money, materials, staff and other assets that can be drawn on by a person or organization in order to function effectively."

According to the Cambridge Dictionary, a resource is:

"a useful or valuable possession or quality of a country, organization, or person."

Both of these definitions, do not substantiate for which purpose resource can be utilized, yet, in SHRM, the term resource is typically associated with firm performance. In his resource-based view (which we will later examine more closely) Barney (2002), specifies company resources as:

> *"all assets, capabilities, competencies, organizational processes, firm attributes, information, knowledge, and so forth that are controlled by a firm and that enable the firm to conceive of and implement strategies designed to improve its efficiency and effectiveness."*

It then shows four categories (economic, of human, physical and organizational assets), and proposes human capital as encompassing:

> *"the training, experience, judgement, intelligence, relationships, and insight of individual managers and workers in a firm."*

Another definition that goes even further is the one by Jackson and Schuler (2006), who state that human resources comprise not only the current employees, but also those who have worked or those who might one day will be working for the company.

However, the implicit problem with the concept of human resource is, that people can be perceived in such a way that they are considered as objects that can be traded as if they were other resources on the market (Martin, 2003).

But, when considering people as human resources, the consequence is that these resources have a type of special needs that must be considered and, therefore, human resources must be managed in a different way (Brewster and Larsen, 2000).

In this sense, human resources are considered as active subjects who cannot be possessed by firms, who are mobile, who have a will of their own with specific aims, and who individually need time to relax and rejuvenate, in order to be a productive member of the organization.

Boxall (2014), also noticed that, in several papers of the last 30 years, human resources were wrongfully defined as people who work in an organization. In another article, he stated that human resources should be regarded as the intrinsic resources that we are endowed with as human beings, which we can use for the different tasks in our lives, in our workplace, as well as in leisure time activities. He specifies his statement by explaining that, if you lose everything, you own what you still have is your knowledge, your experience, your proficiency and, reinforcing these, your physical and emotional condition, intellectual capabilities, personality and motivations.

On that account, human resources are concealed and visible talents that distinguish human beings from other species. As a consequence, human capabilities are crucial to envisaging, furthering and extending organizations, and thus, make them rather distinctive.

As for this book, the definition by Jackson and Schuler is considered to be expedient, because it illustrates the fact that human resources with regard to strategy are of crucial significance for HRM.

2.1.3. Strategic Human Resource Management (SHRM).

As we have seen in the subchapter on strategy definition, we cannot find an unanimously accepted meaning on what strategies are, and how they are being planned. However, in SHRM studies, the predominant opinion refers to strategy as a plan or script to be followed. For example, Wright and McMahan (1992) define SHRM as:

"the pattern of planned human resource deployments and activities intended to enable the firm to achieve its goals."

The fact that this definition does not incorporate emerging strategies and define SHRM from the point of view of strategic planning, is obvious. According to Wright (1998), the above definition focuses on people as a primary source of competitive advantage, both in business practices (to achieve those competitive advantages), and in the attainment of goals. In most of the definitions, SHRM is directly aimed at realizing objectives, which are mostly associated with financial performance and organizational efficacy. A more integrative view comes from Martín Alcázar et al. (2005), defining SHRM as:

"the integrated set of practices, policies and strategies through which organizations manage their human capital, that influences and is influenced by the business strategy, the organizational context and the socio-economic context."

Incorporating the management point of view in human resources, Brewster and Larsen (2000) suggest the use of management in HRM according to "understanding and affecting" relationships between individuals, tasks and organizations. This notion of an understanding and affecting relationship, complies with what is conceived of as Sustainable HRM, which is the reason why this understanding is employed.

2.2. Points of View in SHRM.

Interest in the area of SHRM has steadily increased since the mid-1980s. For this reason, actually we can find an immense amount of studies on the subject. In this subsection, the focus will be on different approaches in the realm of SHRM, in order to establish a basis of understanding for the forthcoming parts of this book. The author is aware that there are other concepts, however, for the purpose of this book, it seems plausible to concentrate on the most popular ones.

2.2.1. Best Fit.

In probably one of the most quoted sources, Baid and Meshoulam (1988) stated that HR activities, such as systems and structures, must match the organization's degree of development, the so-called external fit. This comprises on the one hand casual and more flexible ways of HRM among start-up firms, and more formal and sophisticated forms of HRM as companies grow and expand their workforce.

It also implies that firms in their growth and diversification processes, have to get along with complexity regarding, decentralization and coordination issues of that process. Moreover, apart from the external fit, there is also an internal fit for the need to make sure that individual HR policies are conceptualized to get along and assist each other.

However, the best-fit model with the most extensive reach, has been one in which external fit is described by the competitive business strategy, and not necessarily by the degree of development. In 1987, Schuler and Jackson introduced a model in which they claim that, for SHRM, it is essential to align HR strategy and business needs. Further, they argue that HR practices should be outlined to emphasize the behavioral implications of the different generic strategies determined by Porter. Consequently, this will result in an increase in the performance of a company.

"when HR practices mutually reinforce the firm's (predetermined) choice of cost leadership, differentiation or focus as its competitive posture."

However, the idea that HR practices should be impelled by competitive strategy has been criticized. Firstly, it is argued that the model is not able to detect the need to bring in line employee interests, with the company or adhere to effective social norms and legal specifications during this process. Even though the employer is mostly in a better negotiating position, the leadership staff should offer some ideas how they can ensure that employees are taken care of, because their skills are the key to a firm's success and, consequently, to a firm's survival.

Another critical factor, is the question that the model is not yet sufficiently developed to define a competitive strategy. According to Miller (1992), competitive strategy is often multidimensional, and varies significantly with respect to the business sector. Therefore, it would be quite irrational if HR strategies implied behavioral issues, and HR policies form a competitive strategy that, simply, doesn't fit into the respective industry.

Lastly, it is noted that the model does not pay enough attention to dynamics. While firms take into account the human dimension of any competitive strategy, the constant alteration processes of the economic settings require firms to invest more than that. Briefly summarized, this means that, HR strategy, should be oriented towards the company's current competitive objectives, by hiring and encouraging individuals, with that kind of skill set and commitment needed in the firm's industry. Nevertheless, HR strategy should promote the employees to think outside of the box, and assist in developing those competences that are beneficial for new business ideas, technological progress or alterations in customer expectations. However, it has to be said that, the spills on the approach, do not mean that it is not the most suitable, but that they have to be used in a constructive way to continue with the development, improvement and improvement of all the models in this area of research work.

The main issue though with the models in SHRM, is that scholars often take only two variables into consideration, and try to identify correlations between the two of them. But what is missing here is the complexity of strategic management in reality. This does not mean that researchers are forced to explain every little detail of their models. However, it is true that it is necessary to develop models that are adequate to explain a wide variety of important interrelationships and interlinkages.

Having this said, we should briefly mention Boxall's (1996,1999) approach of a contingency theory, where:

"business strategy is seen as a 'Gestalt' of critical, interdependent elements."

In these elements, central aspects like sectoral choice, competitive strategy, appropriate technology and structure, and essential levels of finance and human capital are encompassed. Thus, a more competitive business strategy, is one that is able to unite all of these integral parts in a more effective configuration, which is then called gestalt.

2.2.2. Best Practice.

Apart from researchers who defend contingency theory, there are writers who think that organizations, should follow best practice procedures regardless of the circumstances.

These writers, are convinced that companies will experience performance improvements, simply, by identifying and adopting proven methods. Especially, in the United States there has been high interest in best practice. In 1994, Jeffery Pfeffer developed sixteen best practice factors, which were later (in 1998) coordinated with seven other principles, including job security, recruitment selection, self-managed teams or teamwork, high salaries dependent on company development, integral training, and reduction of differentials in status and feedback.

Definitions of best practice, can often be traced back to research on the most common functions of personnel psychology, which are selection, training, appraisal and pay.

However, in many cases, this research is too narrow, and combined by writers who are not capable of identifying their values and fail to see the bigger picture. In addition, these collections of good practices, often do not take into account issues, such as work organisation and employee opinion on the subject. Nonetheless, best practices are commonly accepted and quite popular among scholars and practitioners. Although best practice lists vary substantially with regard to the preferable practices, supporters of the best practice approach still continue to distort the question of objectives and interests.

Legge (1978), has already identified the question of what aims are being attended to by best practices, as a problem in the field of business literature. With regard to viability and sustained competitive advantage, the question remains whether best practices are beneficial for either viability, or sustained advantage. If proved methods serve the viability aspect, this means that all the companies in the respective business sector, need to adopt these methods in order to remain viable. If, however, best practices are meant to generate sustained advantage, only few firms will be able to realize it while others will fail.

Still, the questions whose objectives and interests, are being attended to needs to be addressed. In case best practices serves the shareholders as well as the workforce, then there is nothing which speaks against implementing them. Correspondingly, when these proved methods turn out to be harmful for involved parties, one should refrain from adopting them. Yet, what happens if a practice is beneficial for returns but harmful for the employees? Does the workforce have a say in company decisions? And what happens, if a procedure is good for the management staff, but not for either the shareholders or the workforce? These are questions that considerably lead us to scrutinize the idea of best practice approach.

Before questioning the best practice theory, it is worthwhile to take a look at the research evidence. At this point, we should remember the essential difference between descriptive research and normative theory. One of the most obvious aspects, is the remarkable evidence against a universal set of HR practices due to national variations in culture, market regulation and management traditions.

Cultural norms and the exclusive history of different countries, always draw distinctions to the HR management methods, if not even to the objectives of employers for efficiency and revenue. For instance, while capitalist companies share very similar objectives all over the world, they substantially adapt to local opinions, customs and laws in their quest for shareholder well-being which is, of course, more than comprehensible. So, diversity in HR practices due to societal implications is one aspect, however, there is growing variety with regard to research on the prevalence of best practices in any capitalist country.

But, why is there a problem of diffusion, if there are proved methods, and why don't more companies implement them? In one of the rare studies on best practices, Ostermann (1994) found out that more than a third of US private sector institutions with more than 50 employees, have actually implemented such best practice methods. But he also highlights that, sectoral and organizational variables, are more essential in explaining why some companies have implemented more of these methods than others.

Companies that are more likely to implement proved methods, are those that are involved in international competition, utilize sophisticated technology, and engage in competitive strategies that include a well-balanced mixture of quality and service dimensions as well as expenses.

Other experts, such as Weinstein and Kochan (1995), draw the same conclusion as they state that implementation of key changes is more widely disseminated in emerging firms than in already existing organizations, as well as in rather larger than smaller enterprises, and in technically more sophisticated branches such as automotive, telecommunications or information technology than in for instance the clothing industry.

In general, the US research proposes that best practices are more popular in branches where quality and service play a major role, and where companies can only remain viable, if they are capable of taking advantage of sophisticated technology or professional service. In business sectors where these circumstances cannot be fulfilled, firms adhere to more simple employment methods, that allow focusing on recruiting and retaining sufficient employees in the respective sector. In loose labor markets, this means that working conditions have not shown any dynamics. In fact, there is not much research that can be utilized to affirm a general case for any of the lists of proven methods wheresoever. Therefore, the implementation of best practices should be treated cautiously.

As has been noted before, descriptive research shows that HR practices are ineluctable contingent on coherence, including social, sectoral and organizational issues. But does this mean that all the ideas on best practice theory are nullified? Or is there still a raison d'être for the best practice approach? Boxall and Purcell at this point propose a distinction between:

"the top layer of policy and practice and the underpinning layer of principle and process."

They argue that hardly any compilation of best practices will have universal relevance, however, principles and processes are another topic. If we reflect upon the vast research on employment relations, it is quite obvious that under identical conditions, all institutions are better off when they strive after certain principles.

In HR management, the most important principle is the persistent need to adjust leadership and employee interests in organizations, at least at the level of a contract that serves the minimum requirements of the parties involved. Moreover, organizational processes that enhance the trust between management personnel and workforce, will eventually ensure better outcomes for both parties.

In general, it is always better to offer people the chance to collaborate in the policy development process, than to make decisions without having previously heard their opinion. And, of course, it is always beneficial if the management keeps up to its promise, because any inconsistency between HR policy and HR practice will ultimately destroy the trust of the workforce in their management.

Nevertheless, the past has shown that the principles of best practice do not necessarily sustain indefinitely or can be applied as desirable to all occupational groups.

There are economic disruptions, such as growing competition that lead to compromises between management and workforce damaging trust relations, and further dividing the workforce between highly skilled and valuable employees and the common less skilled manpower, in more or less insecure employment relationships. In a nutshell, we can note that there are some best practice methods for HR management, but the principles firms implement to realize their performance objectives are strongly dependent on societal, sectoral and organizational aspects.

2.2.3. Perspective of the company according to the resources.

The introduction of the company's resource-based perspective (RBV) in the area of SHRM research was very positively received by the scientific community, and has influenced this field of research in many ways.

Early beginnings of the RBV can be traced back to Edith Penrose, who in the late 1950s argued that the firm consists of an administrative organization and an accumulation of productive resources. She differentiated between physical and human resources, and included the knowledge and the experience of the management into the term human resources into her concept.

In contrast to the neo-classical approach, where firms within industries are considered homogenous, the RBV understands that competition is not able to wipe away:

"all differences among firms in the same line of business".

The limitations of factor markets become apparent when firms are defined as unique bundles of resources, because we then see that some factors that firms need can be acquired in the market, but others can only be developed within the firm itself. In this context, each firm then creates its own set of factors which is hardly imitable.

For experts in the study of strategy, the most interesting factor is therefore to find the key to how companies may be able to develop exclusive, own and desirable sets of resources and human and technical assets. The value of the resources can be recovered by the fact that, in any situation in which the market finds itself, a competitive company will be able to take advantage of the current circumstances, or face threats more or less freely, while the rival company will not be able to do so.

Therefore, the company that has the advantages must know how to manage these scarce resources in a way that the competitors are frustrated and tired, of trying to follow the pace of the other stronger company. Naturally, nobody and nothing is immune against unexpected developments that have a disarranging impact (sometimes also called Schumpeterian Shocks) on the respective business sector; however, there is some room for firms to differentiate themselves in a competitive situation in a rather viable way.

The main focus in the RBV is then to figure out how firms are able to separate rare resources from eroding, whereof basically the competition in capitalist economies consists of. In this context, in their article Boxall and Purcell (2000), have summarized some aspects that are regarded as crucial with regard to the issue of developing viable competitive advantage. The first one refers to unique timing and learning. Experts in the field, highlight the way in which scarce resources are built over time, not only through mostly golden opportunities, but also through smart people who gather together, and approach vital business occasions when they arise with a combination of their talent and other key resources. Boxall and Purcell postulate that:

> "a combination of unique timing and learning is the fundamental 'barrier to imitation' or 'isolating mechanism'"

Another aspect is social complexity. In the course of firm growth, firms develop multifaceted structures of coordination, communication systems and different aspects of teamwork that are exclusive to the respective firm. These unique social structures and interconnections, can be seen as natural obstacles to copying by rivals. Maintaining an advantage through these social structures is one of the main tasks in the objectives of the human resources strategy, how the company is able to match business interests with qualified employees and develop their skills in the long term.

The last issue identified in this realm is causal ambiguity. Similar to social complexity, ambiguity about the cause-effect relationships encompassed in the firm's performance, is an unavoidable outcome of company growth. Yet, the extent of causal ambiguity is mutable. Typically, there is more uncertainty about the reasons of high performance in the rivals' minds, however, it is argued that this is perhaps overestimated in respect of managers within the company that is leading amongst the competitors.

Taking all these factors into account, theorists suggest that higher degrees of peculiarity among companies, offer the possibility for generating viable competitive advantage. However, one should be cautious with stressing the idea of differentiation too much, because it might be misleading. It is quite easy to emphasize the differences between companies in the same business sector, but in the same business sector all the firms need quite similar resources in order to be competitive.

These basic requirements, include the guidelines and minimum human resources standards that each company must adopt, in order to play a decisive role in the market. Obviously, the question of the minimum with respect to the human resources system depends on the business environment. The crucial aspect at this point is, that viable companies are not totally peculiar or distinctive, but only partially.

This means that the effort is to disclose differences and commonalities, and to describe which are the aspects that help the company to acquire and maintain sustained competitive advantage over its competitors, and how and why some companies are successful in their endeavors and others fail.

A fairly popular approach to VBR is associated with the investigation of Hamel and Prahalad (1993/94), who claim that competitive strength over a long period of time is derived from the creation of "core competencies" in enterprise, which are sharper than those of rivals. Hamel and Prahalad have developed a model which is especially essential for higher management staff, because it offers recommended actions that enable the leaders of companies to figure out the subjacent structures, and clusters of knowledge in their very own company:

"that transcend the artificial divisions of 'strategic business units' or might do so if they were appropriately managed."

Leonard (1992, 1998), offers quite an alike framework that assists leaders to disclose those core competencies with regard to firm's products and services. In her framework, the core competencies are named 'knowledge sets', that consist of four dimensions: the 'content' dimensions, which include relevant skills and know-how of the employees as well as technical systems, and the 'process' dimensions, which include managerial matters and values and norms.

Looking at this framework from an HR perspective, it is probably one of the most supportive approaches. The managerial system includes the crucial HR policies that are necessary to recruit, develop and motivate the workforce, with the respective skills and qualifications. Leonard further stresses that all the dimensions are intertwined, and that there is a bias that those core capabilities might turn into inflexibility, if the company does not learn to regenerate those.

As we have seen, the both very shortly introduced models let us draw the conclusion that it is a company's capability to learn faster, and to adjust its conduct more productively than its competitors, which is what results in competitive advantage.

In that sense, it becomes apparent that questions about the ways in which human capabilities, motives and interactions, play an important role in finding out how to improve organizations with regard to learning and adapting to the volatile markets.

Influenced by the vivid interest in the RBV, strategic HRM researchers, then were eager to figure out how and to what extent HR policies and practices play a role in the uniqueness of the company.

With referring to Barney (1991), Wright et al. (1994) distinguished between the company's human resources (human capital) and HR activities as such. They said that even though a company's pool of human resources can be a sustained competitive edge, it seems almost impossible for HR practices to be limited, not imitable and not interchangeable.

The role that HR practices can play, is described as generating the pool of human resources and motivating human attitude traits, which really make a difference and lead to an advantage. Other companies may be able to imitate HR practices, however, if they do not have the quality of the employees' talent, they will not be able to participate in the competition, as they are the superior company in terms of the best resources.

Thus, the leading company then has acquired a prime mover advantage in HRM. In this case, as Kamoche (1996) and Coff (1997) note, it becomes a challenge for the superior company to keep their highly developed workforce, if it is to maintain an advantage and cope successfully with the problem of practicability, which is that of receiving valuable returns to the firm from the workforce.

Unlike what Wright et al. (1994) postulated, Lado and Wilson (1994) suggested that the source of the company's continuous competitive advantage is based on human resource performance. Referring to the concept of exploring the role of human resources that impact on the company's capabilities, they proposed that human resources systems can be unique, causally unclear, and synergistic in the way they enhance the company's capabilities, and therefore could hardly be imitated. Accordingly, while Wright et al. (1994) stressed the imitability of individual employee behavior, Lado and Wilson considered the HR system with all its interrelations to be the main aspect of possible imitation, in order to generate sustained competitive advantage.

In 1992, Cappelli and Singh provided a review of the impact of RBV on SHRM. They observed that most of the SHRM models based on fit suppose that a specific business strategy asks for an exclusive set of employee conduct and that particular HR policies induce an exclusive set of employee responses. They also reasoned that it seems easier to reorganize resources if given a certain strategy than it is to reorganize the strategy with a given set of resources. Consequently, they suggested the RBV might offer theoretical groundwork for why HR strategy could have impact on as well the strategy formulation and implementation.

According to Mueller (1996), what is more likely to lead to sustained competitive advantage are the minor changes to underlying routines that are rooted in the firm's 'social architecture' – a term that contrary to the word 'culture' describes better the constructive role of deviant behavior. He also recognizes a set of 'resource mobility barriers' that impede competitors from copying such organizational behaviors. Those barriers can be outlined as a continuous, insistent management process that creates useful new skills within the firm's set of resources.

Building on a framework from Mueller (1996), Wright et al. (1994) and others, Boxall (1998, 1999) then takes the next step and distinguishes between 'human capital advantage' and 'organizational process advantage'. Boxall argues that human capital advantage is likely if companies hire individuals with a worthwhile, but at the same time, exceptional set of knowledge and skills, and which are to a certain degree firm-specific.

In addition to that, the advantage of organizational sequences is that it becomes a function, which makes it almost impossible to copy sophisticated processes within the company, e.g. cross-functional learning and collaboration between management and workforce.

Consequently, in order to achieve continuous advantage through people, it is the task of management to foster resources and routines that are capable of creating high reciprocity with talented employees, as well as investing in employee development, both personally and in team.

Another model, introduced by Lepak and Snell (1999), suggested that within organizations there is variance regarding the exclusiveness and value of competencies.

Another model, developed by Lepak and Snell (1999), advised that within companies there are differences in the exclusivity and value of skills. By contrasting these two extremes with each other, they realized that some employees are more prone to competitive advantage than others. This implies that they will also have to be managed differently.

Their findings also led to a greater awareness among SHRM researchers of the fact that there is a variety of HR practices within a company, and that seeking an HR strategy could conceal important differences in the types of human capital available to companies.

Having summarized the most popular conceptual and theoretical aspects of VBR in SHRM theories, the next step is to check what has been tested within empirical research. Here, three exemplary studies are going to be recapitulated.

In general, Huselid believed that human resource practices could be effective in creating a source of competitive advantage, especially if embedded in the gearing of business strategy. His study at the time showed a close relationship between HR practices and employee turnover, the gross asset productivity rate and Tobin's Q.

The study also found that there was a strong correlation between HR practices and employee turnover, the gross asset productivity rate and Tobin's Q. This attracted a lot of interest because it showed that HR practices could really have a solid influence on accounting and key performance and productivity indicators.

A similar approach was applied by Koch and McGrath (1996), in their research on the correlation between human resource planning, hiring and staffing procedures, and work effectiveness. They said that prolific employees most probably possess a specific skill set that render the workforce an extremely worthwhile strategic asset. Further, they proposed that companies that elaborate a sophisticated routine in hiring people, also elaborate a pool of talents which is almost inimitable.

Another study conducted by Boxall and Steeneveld (1999), examined whether any firms in the sample have set any kind of sustained competitive advantage over competitors, due to better HR strategy. They proposed that one of the companies has acquired a better competitive position, because of an advantage in human resources in a particular year, but found out that a couple of years later the two rivals had equaled out.

For the researchers, this implied that either the two companies were capable of successfully copying the former superior's firm human resources advantage, or that the previously superior competitor has elaborated an advantage which he wasn't aware of in the beginning, but which will be capitalized over the long run.

This point again reinforces the issue that companies need certain forms of alike human resources just to be able to exist in the particular business sector. The study reveals that companies are most likely to survive economic crises only in a competition with timely and effective leadership succession. Moreover, it confirms Mueller's (1996) point of view that is quite time-consuming and a special motivation to establish organizational routines that provide the sustained competitive advantage.

As can be proved, the empirical implementation of VBR changes in its format, moving the focus of HR practices and talent groups towards matching the skill set of the labour force and strategy, but still provides a common basic logic behind all these orientations: it is believed that human resource activities foster skilled and talented employees and this entire workforce will be motivated to be involved in functional performance behavior for the company.

Consequently, these HR activities are a source of competitive advantage that translates into increased operational output, which can be transformed into higher profitability and later into higher market value.

3. The Idea of Sustainability in HRM.

3.1. Definitions.

Similar to the preceding chapter, some meanings of certain important terms, will be explained to ensure that the reader has the same comprehensive understanding of the terms drawn as the writer of this book.

3.1.1. Sustainability.

The terms sustainable or sustainability are often used synonymously for words like for instance durable, long-term, future-proof or viable to just name a few and they nowadays have become crucial for the world in general and business in particular.
As early as 1987, the United Nations World Commission on Environment and Development, also known as the "Brundtland Commission," published a report describing sustainable development as a:

> *"development that meets the needs of the present without compromising the ability of future generations to meet their own needs"*

and, in this environment, has aroused growing attention in the field of business management and, in the last few years, also in that of human resources management.
The main objective pursued by the Brundtland Commission in publishing this document was to produce:

> *"an agenda for global change and a common future for mankind and has been concerned with the question of how to advance societal and economic development without endangering natural living conditions for the majority of humanity."*

The Commission also commented that sustainable development at the community level requires the implementation of the economic, ecological and social components of sustainability at the same time.

With this regard, in the 1990s the so-called triple-bottom-line model emerged obliging organizations to define also environmental and societal objectives apart from merely financial profits.

With this Brundtland Commission's definition, quite a few alternative interpretations of concepts dealing with the responsibilities of business have evolved. Although the concept of corporate sustainability (CS), as such is not the main focus of this book, it is worthwhile to contemplate this idea since there is existing agreement that it

> *"refers to some composite and multi-faceted construct that entails environmental, social, and economic organizational outcomes."*

Still, researchers on CS, haven't offered a definition that extends the win-win-win thinking based on the triple-bottom-line. In fact, win-win-win situations might be achievable in certain companies and certain environments; however, for the most part of the organizations, it will be particularly challenging to generate economic, ecological benefits, and social and human sustainability, at the same time without reconsidering their business strategy and organizational structure all over again.

Another possibility of interpreting sustainability is to contextualize it with businesses, acting in neoliberal environments, rather than providing an array of stakeholder interests. In this case, one stakeholder – for the most part the shareholders – is being favored, and it is asserted that managers and executives are the instruments of the shareholders, and consequently above all liable to them. This means that all actions regarding the business are coordinated with the shareholders' intentions, which means to make as much financial benefit as possible whilst adhering to laws and regulations.

To get to the bottom of this interpretation, we can say that this conception of sustainability is based on the premise that market mechanisms will allocate rare resources in the best possible way. As a result, managers and executives are not responsible for results beyond the short- and long-term cash results that are profitable for the company's shareholders. Thus, actions in the realm of social responsibility, for instance investments in facilities, are delineated only to promote financial benefits of the company.

In this sense, these actions are carried out to improve the sustainability of the company and, in short, to constitute a benefit for shareholders. Yet, since the focus is on the shareholders, negative impacts on the stakeholders (e.g. employees, future generations) are not considered in this approach. Rather organizational survival and viability are the main focus.

As we have seen previously, the notion of sustainability in the area of human resources management is still a little scarce and quite difficult to understand.

As part of his study, Ehnert (2009, pp.62-67) has identified ways of understanding sustainability that offer an effective way of seeing the connection between sustainability and HRM. It distinguishes between a normative view, oriented towards efficacy and innovation, and a subject-oriented view of the relationship between sustainability and human resource management.

The normative understanding of sustainability, reaffirms the Brundtland Commission's definition of sustainable development at the business level, and yet this definition, has been formulated to improve the quality of life of the world's citizens, to reduce the problem that, many global resources, are exploited by industrialised countries to improve their prosperity, and to invest in the situation of future generations and the least developed countries, as they do not have the same opportunities to generate wealth.

In this sense, sustainability is seen as the solution to the problem of intergenerational and intragenerational equality. Therefore, the main point of normative comprehension of sustainability is that responsibility towards a range of parties is seen as an end in itself and not as progress in the financial interests of a company's shareholders.

The efficiency- and innovation-oriented comprehension of sustainability is rooted in the debate on environmental management. Companies that aim to do less harm to the environment try to combine this objective with financial aspirations such as cost reduction or value creation and thus try to achieve a sustained competitive advantage for their organisation. In short, the goal of understanding sustainability oriented to effectiveness and innovation is to reduce costs, or improve the efficacy of the use of assets and the creation of value through innovation.

Substance-oriented comprehension is a totally different view of the term sustainability and goes back to Aristotle's view of a home and the beginning of forestry. Following this view, a firm acts, sustainably and economically rational if the ratio of resource reproduction and resource consumption equals one. This concept of sustainability originates in the old forest laws that existed in Europe, which held the theory that, to maintain a level of wood supply, consumption and reproduction must also be in the same quantity. As far as human resources management is concerned, this means that this viewpoint aims to take care of the organisational resources and, in particular, the human resources of a firm in order to survive in the future. Therefore, organizations need to be aware of the importance of employee value and quality.

3.1.2. Management of a sustainable form of resources.

The notion of introducing the Sustainable Resource Management (SRM) viewpoint, as an example of another perception of the relationship between sustainability and HRM, is based on the difficulty of addressing the problem of labour shortages; or in other words, the limited availability of human resources.

The SRM concept illustrates how companies manage their resources, and approaches the question of how corporate resources originate ("source of the resources"), focusing on where the emergence of resources is, as well as, on the matter of how this emergence can be affected beforehand, rather than only reacting ex post to changes in business settings.

The aim of this term is to offer a different paradigm in management philosophy, and to define a new rationality, i.e. sustainability, to confront corporate resources. The approach, also seeks to explain resource shortage with a disruption in the origin of resources, which is believed to be triggered by the organizations themselves, because of the influence they have on their surroundings. Yet, these surroundings are not considered as restrictions, but rather as sources of resources.

It is therefore imperative, that these resource sources have to remain at their levels, in order to allow for the continued and perennial use of significant resources.

The objective is to maintain a constant interaction between enterprises and their environment, because it is supposed that interdependencies are so strong, that in the long term the common sustainability of organizations, and their environments seems to be the only option.

Thus, if companies comprehend that they are only able of surviving together with their environments, investing in these environments, becomes a plausible course of action. In this sense, as organizations and their surroundings are interpreted as a "resource community" or "survival community", the SRM concept pursues the idea of scrutinizing a causal explanation for the interdependencies between companies and their environments.

Nevertheless, utilizing and replicating human resources at the same time, represents a challenge for HR practitioners, since they are facing a dilemma: efficiency and sustainability. Thus, Ehnert (2009) recommends that

"resource exploitations follow the economic logic of efficiency and that reproduction has to follow the logic of sustainability."

3.1.3. Sustainable HRM.

The expression Sustainable Human Resource Management has been employed for more than a couple of years; however, the bibliography on this matter is scarce, as research in this area is at an early or even incipient stage and, due to the lack of a commonly accepted accurate definition, researchers and professionals face problems when treating the subject, as the expression has been used in multiple ways.

The first contributions on this theme arose in the late 1990s in Germany, by Müller Christ and Remer (1999), who found that, not only natural but also human resources, are in many instances scarce resources that are crucial to the viability of organizations, and therefore, defined sustainable human resource management as:

> *"what organizations themselves have to do in their environments to have access to highly qualified people in the future (p.76; translated from German by the authors)"*.

Others (e.g. Wilkinson et al., 2001), affirmed that resource and human resource management methods are frequently too short-term oriented and, therefore, unsuccessful, and that people in enterprises are more or less worked (or burned out) than developed and proficient.

The first systematically, theoretically and empirically recognised viewpoint on sustainable human resource management, was proposed by Swiss academics (Thom, Schüpbach-Brönnimann, Zaugg), who noticed that more and more Swiss corporations have problems finding highly qualified and involved people, and that an increasing number of workers are unable to work due to stress-related concerns, according to Ehnert (2009).

This view of Sustainable Human Resource Management, addresses the definition of the Brundtland Commission. Investigators consider employees as self-sustaining human resources, who carry out all HR activities together with HR staff and line managers, and understand HRM's role as a guardian of human resources.

In addition, they presuppose that companies, employees and society are all responsible for Sustainable Human Resource Management tasks. As human resources are seen as self-responsible, it is presumed that they are responsible for themselves, and also in control of their careers including goals such as employability, work-life balance, participating in the decision-making process and well-being.

In this environment, sustainability is understood as a shared reward for all policyholders and supports long-term financial sustainability. However, economic success by itself is not the key to viability of the organization. Indeed, by dealing with human beings in a sustainable way, it is believed to generate sustained competitive advantage. Consequently, the definition offered by Zaugg et al. (2001), outlining Sustainable HRM as:

> *"long term socially and economically efficient recruitment, development, retainment and disemployment of employees"*

seems plausible. In the meantime, Gollan (2005) characterized:

> *"human resource sustainability in terms of the capacity of organizations to create value, thereby having the ability capacity to regenerate value and renew wealth through the application of human resource policies and practices".*

A more recent definition on Sustainable HRM was offered by Cohen et al. (2012) who stated:

"Sustainable HRM is the utilization of HR tools to help embed a sustainability strategy in the organization and the creation of an HRM system that contributes to the sustainable performance of the firm. Sustainable HRM creates the skills, motivation, values and trust to achieve a triple bottom line and at the same time ensures the long-term health and sustainability of both the organization's internal and external stakeholders, with policies that reflect equity, development and well-being and help support environmentally friendly practices."

Under this definition, the principal goals of sustainable human resource management are equal treatment (equity), worker development and wellness, and environmentally respectful business processes. In this sense, it is not considered to be sustainable if at work one is confronted with psychological stress, women and men are paid unequally and if females are represented disproportionately lower than their male colleagues.

It can be observed that in the definitions provided, there are distinctions with respect to the goals of Sustainable Human Resources Management and, moreover, the literature on Sustainable Human Resources Management varies with respect to the significance given to the desired internal and external results. Writers on sustainable HRM have linked different notions and ideas of sustainability with HRM, for instance, sustainable work systems, sustainable leadership, and sustainable organization. Although these terms approach the effort to harmonize financial goals, social and ecological factors in different ways, all of which are centred on the human and social result of the company.

The following subchapter will further examine the different perspectives on sustainable human resources management and introduce their main findings.

3.2. Approaches in Sustainable HRM.

As the research on Sustainable HRM is still in an emerging phase, the literature on this topic is for the time being quite manageable. However, Ehnert and Harry (2012), and Kramar (2014), found out there have been different stages or waves in the development of research in the field which they clustered into three groups. In the following subchapters we are going to have a closer look on these categories, respectively approaches in Sustainable HRM.

3.2.1. Capability Reproduction.

In the literature on Sustainable HRM, an essential part of papers deals with linking HRM practices with internal, especially economic outcomes. As we can see from the research, the SHRM framework proves that HRM processes have a positive impact on the company's financial results, through mediating elements that reflect human results (such as job fulfilment).
Unlike SHRM's bibliography, specialists in Sustainable Human Resource Management, who explicitly highlight business results, have recognized economic and social or human results as results of the organization's performance. In particular, they concentrate on the promotion of economic performance and the long-term sustainability of the organization through the implementation of human resource management, that have a positive impact on social or human results.

As believed by those writers, the Sustainable HRM concept stands for a new integral approach to people management, and can be interpreted as an extension of SHRM. In this approach, it is postulated that certain HRM practices are crucial for the advancement of the human capabilities that are necessary to work in surroundings facing environmental, demographic and social constraints. In this context, Ehnert (2009) offers a definition on Sustainable HRM which acknowledges the existence of duality. She asserts:

"Sustainable HRM is the pattern of planned or emerging human resource strategies and practices intended to enable organizational goal achievement while simultaneously reproducing the HR base over a long-lasting calendar time and controlling for self-induced side and feedback effects of HR systems on the HR base and thus on the company itself."

So, according to Ehnert, the principal goals of sustainable human resources management are, firstly, to balance the vagueness and duality of effectiveness and sustainability in a long-term view; secondly, to uphold, promote and reproduce the human and social resource base of the company, which means supporting reciprocal terms of trade; and, thirdly, to identify and determine the negative effects of human resources actions on the human resource base. Unlike previous definitions where the main focus was on outcomes, this definition also takes into account the processes entailed in Sustainable HRM.

Therefore, sustainable HR implies that an agency is an open standard with the need to move ahead and reproduce its human resources, at least as quickly as it uses them. As the dualities and dilemmas for HR specialists in Sustainable Human Resource Management have been realised, professionals face the need to push for efficiency, and invest in advancing human skills simultaneously. In addition, executives need to be conscious of the interdependence of the organization's surroundings and resources.

Some of the papers in this field of research also seem to be quite similar to HRM bundles such as high-performance works systems or high-performance work practices, rather than depicting new methods of people management.

The main distinction between those models and Sustainable HRM, though, is that in Sustainable HRM the central concerns are long-term social and human outcomes. So, some experts affirm that HR sustainability calls for a shift of focus from rather short-term viability of the organization to long-term longevity, and a focus on positive personnel outcomes.

At the same time, the importance of the debate on sustainability in HR has been pointed out in the field of sustainable work systems, which is quite connected and has its origins in organisational conduct and working relationships.

In this field, academics explore how constructively and experientially unions are able to evolve and sustain work systems that are sustainable with respect to economic, ecological and social aspects and that promote recovery, health and human progress (see, for example, Docherty et al., 2002, 2009; Kira, 2002; Moldaschl & Fischer, 2004).

They are eager to identify negative human and social results at the individual, organizational and social levels, and to set up sustainable work systems that result in the achievement of the transformation, and furtherance of the organization's human and social capital.

They also recognize the detrimental effects of human resource policies, such as overtime work, short-term employment, disproportionate performance standards, etc. on the well-being and satisfaction of individual employees. The development of HR practices that result in positive human results, e.g. work-life balance, as well as the organization's financial performance and sustainable change procedures, are of great importance to this group of academics. At this point, with the focus being human regeneration, health and furtherance, we notice an overlapping with literature on Sustainable HRM.

3.2.2. Promoting Social and Environmental Health.

Another group of researchers (for instance, Mariappanadar, 2003, 2012; Orlitzky et al. 2003; Branco and Rodrigues 2006; Collinson et al 2007) in the field of HRM sustainability, discovered that there is a connection between human resource management, and external results that are associated with Corporate Social Responsibility (CSR) and the triple bottom line.

As an important part of the bibliography, it finds out how human and social and/or area, results play a role in economic and financial results. Authors on the topic tend to look at the efficiency-oriented focus of sustainability. As noted above, the term sustainable human resource management is used to refer to human resource management processes that help achieve positive ecological/environmental and social/human results, with the intention of obtaining financial success.

Companies demonstrating good social and ecological practices, have been found to positively influence the company's financial performance. Moreover, firms that invest in ethical issues, display even better financial results than others, whereas markets recompense businesses that are aware of the environment.

This importance of the economic results of social and ecological outcomes is considered when assessing practitioners' understanding of sustainability in HRM. For example, in a research study by Zaugg, Blum and Thom (2001) on the understanding of sustainability in HRM by HR professionals it has been shown that economics outcomes were given priority.

Researchers also have presented different views on the concept of sustainability in HRM, by transferring this idea to certain HR issues, like HR strategy for mitigating problems with regard to downsizing activities (Mariappanadar, 2003, 2012; Wilkinson, 2005), the impact of sustainability on talent performance (Boudreau & Ramstad, 2005), the relevance of human sustainability (Pfeffer, 2010; Scholz & Müller, 2010,Z. ink, 2008) and a stakeholder focus on Sustainable Human Resource Management (Guerci, 2011).

At this point it is noticeable that Pfeffer asserts that in the social debate on ecologization and sustainability, human sustainability is more or less ignored.

Also, in this context, papers can be found that deal with the outcomes of HRM on external effects, especially with regard to social and human aspects. These results include family and social wealth, worker wellbeing, policy and government costs. Writers of this group pay essentially close attention to negative externalities, which can be described as,

"something that costs the organization nothing for their actions or business practices, but those business practices are costly to third parties."

Although this accepts the repercussions of HRM's practices on outsiders, it does not address the incidence of HRM's external forces. In this case, attention is called to ignorance of HRM's policies on results other than social and human, notably ecological results.

3.2.3. Connections.

Another body of literature in the sphere of study on Sustainable HRM, can be classified as connections, which means that writers in the field start to work in interdisciplinary teams, and that they focus on the interrelations between management practices and organizational outcomes, including environmental, social and financial outcomes.

Therefore, the social debate on sustainability is at the centre of awareness. And, as a moral question can be raised about organizations that behave responsibly, more attention is paid to the role of HRM in creating not only economically and socially, but also ecologically sustainable and responsible organizations (take a look, for instance Cohen et al., 2012; Clarke, 2011; Müller-Camen et al., 2008).

However, it has been observed that writers often neglect to look into the sustainability idea with all its facets, as a whole with the consequence that competing concepts, such as for instance Green HRM or Socially Responsible HRM emerge. Although Green HRM concentrates principally on the environmental sustainability of HRM, recognizing the superiority of economic results, Socially Responsible HRM aims more at reflecting on social sustainability and CSR.

There is also literature on sustainable leadership that recognizes the fact that management methods differ depending on national context (e.g. Avery and Bergsteiner, 2010). Publications on change for sustainability and sustainable organizations (Dunphy et al., 2007) and publications on green HRM (Renwick, Redman and Maguire, 2011) identify the interlinkages between environmental performance and HRM and other management systems.

It has been demonstrated that environmental and human/social results are both linked, and support the sustainability of the company. The advancement and enforcement of environmental policies are subject to the establishment of HRM procedures, that evoke trust between the workforce, management personnel and the respective surroundings of the organization. In this context, Dunphy et al. (2007) came up with a six-stage model that stands for different stages of sustainability, and defined these six stages as: expulsion, lack of response, fulfillment, efficacy, strategic pro-activity and the sustaining agency. They stated that a sustaining organization is an organization:

"which fully incorporates the tenets of human and ecological sustainability into its own operations"

and also encourages to apply this understanding of sustainability more widely. Such an organization, as it is described by Dunphy et al. (2007), is distinguished by strong corporative assets and senior executive coaching with flexible frameworks and human resource management practices, that build employee skills, integrate the labour force into decision-making exercises, guarantee diversity management, and address health and safety aspects of ethical issues.

With respect to Green Human Resources Management, or sometimes also called GHRM, it should be mentioned that, the connection between environmental management and Human Resources Management, is the main focus in this case, and can be considered as an extension of Human Resources Management, as it involves sustainability issues, and approaches the role of Human Resources Management in environmental performance in a similar manner (e.g. Kramar, 2012; Jackson et al., 2011, Renwick et al., 2011).

In this context, Renwick et al. (2011) stated more precisely that an array of HRM policies (recruiting, training, performance governance, remuneration and recompense system, etc.) have been identified to set up the framework, that is necessary to generate positive environmental outcomes.

Since sustainability and aspects of environment protection are inevitable intertwined, it seems reasonable to look more closely into the main features of Green HRM.

As already mentioned in the introduction, increasing pollution and shortage of natural resources motivate more and more organizations to actively engage in the protection of our environment. Ecological issues such as the climate change and energy efficiency, are considered as for one thing as threat, but then again also as a chance with regard to innovation processes. Developing and implementing an ecological environment management in organizations, will then become an important task for the HRM since the central HRM functions (recruiting, performance management, compensation and benefits, etc.) can contribute in various ways to a sustainable and environment-oriented configuration of organizational processes. Also, with regard to recruitment, personnel will be employed that pursues green objectives, and is willing to enhance the company.

In this environment, establishing and maintaining the company as a sustainable business, will gain in significance as employer branding tactics that aim for a green life, and will attract young and highly skilled employees.

In terms of performance management and remuneration, it is indispensable that, in addition to agreements on economic goals, agreements on ecological objectives are negotiated with employees, which can be implemented through benefits directly related to a long-term approach and to the ecological and social performance of the organization.

In the field of Green HRM, human resource development includes, for example, education centred on the enhancement of ecological knowledge, which plays a fundamental role in behavioural change in the sense of sustainable environmental practices. Along with these trainings, it has been shown that ecological sabbaticals in companies (e.g. Patagonia, Wal-Mart, PwC) promote green living at work and at home.

Coming back to the study conducted by Zaugg et al. (2001) in eight European countries (Germany, Italy, Spain, France, Austria, Great Britain, Netherlands, and Switzerland), it has been proved that the national environment is relevant to the sustainable management of human resources, and that in all the countries in which the research was performed, with the exception of Switzerland, sustainability was associated with a drive towards economic targets.

This opinion was derived from the supposition that HR results contribute to financial results and, therefore to, to the longevity of the organization. In the words of Zaugg et al (2001), employees are considered equal members of management, and are regarded as self-responsible parties. The HRM system is then responsible for the advancement of the workforce so that they are beneficial for their families and community.

In light of this, employee development, pay and reward system and the integration of sustainability into the company's guiding principles, is of utmost importance. Considering further the sustainable leadership concept which:

> *"refers to achieving futures in which humans live within their ecological and social means, without exploiting other parties"*

this focus can be seen as an election for people management and a leadership culture that can be taken up in multiple national environments.

4. Differences & Commonalities.

Having delineated the most successful concepts of SHRM and Sustainable Human Resource Management in the preceding chapters, this chapter will compare both these two concepts to get a better impression of where and to what extent differences and similarities can be identified.

Nevertheless, given that research on the theme of sustainability in HRM is still in an initial phase, there are hardly any documents that really take on the challenge of comparing the two concepts. In fact, most writers rather try to find out what Sustainable HRM offers, in addition to already familiar aspects regarding SHRM instead of contrasting both approaches with regard to certain criteria.

This is due to the fact that sustainable human resource management, should not be seen as a completely new discovery in the area of managing people, but instead as an expansion and development of concepts already available in the area of human resource management. The following subchapters will shed light on these issues.

4.1. A Shift of Paradigm.

Proponents of Sustainable HRM consider this new field of research as a shift of paradigm, and a new stage of development in the course of people management. Some authors consider sustainable human resources management to be the fourth phase of human resources management after

> *"workforce administration, staff management and strategic human resources stewardship"*

Others (Kienbaum Management Consultants) see Sustainable HRM as HR 3.0 after coming from State of the art (HR 2.0) and HR basic requirements (HR 1.0) practices.

This next stage of development (HR 3.0) is led by the key question: How can a mutual profitable compensation between employee interests and company interests look like? The main task in this context is to overcome the purely instrumental focus on employees, and to satisfy their interests and demands as stakeholders. Crucial to success is here to create a reciprocal balance of interests.

Regardless of whether people management finds itself in the third or fourth step of development, it should be noted that, talking about a shift of paradigm, seems to be reasonable in this context since there are three essential features that are adopted in HRM.

Firstly, the focus is no longer only on impacts of HRM on financial outcomes of the organization. In fact, social and environmental outcomes of HRM practices are now progressing to become important arguments for the HR function. As a consequence, new fields in HRM, like for instance employee well-being, diversity management, etc. are growing more relevant.

Secondly, considering a higher number of stakeholders, gains in significance. It is no longer enough to meet the needs of owners, managers and employees; but also of other parties, such as environmentalists, clients and providers, different governments, associations, family and friends, etc., who actively contribute to or are affected by human resource performance. New to the lobby, for example, environmentalists are inviting organizations to limit their carbon dioxide emissions, which is one of the ways in which more and more corporations are beginning to address environmental matters, and participate actively in environmental management. In this area, the Office of Human Resources Management of the Greens could play an important role.

Third, the sustainable management of OHRM staff must take into account actions taken outside the limits of the agency. This means that entrepreneurial responsibility has to be extended to, for instance, the supply chain. In particular, due to human rights organizations and other non-governmental organizations, who coerce companies to comply with certain standards, a lot of firms now show interest in the work conditions of their suppliers, especially with regard to HRM practices concerning child labor and jobs associated with health risks. Since dealing with Human Rights issues is one of the core functions of HRM, this HR function has inevitably to be extended to employees in the supply chain.

At this point, since an operationalization of Sustainable HRM has not yet been developed, it is useful to look more closely at the Global Reporting Initiative (GRI) standards, since they offer a promising opportunity to report on sustainability. GRI is an independent international organization that has pioneered sustainability reporting since the late 1990s. As stated on their website:

"GRI helps businesses and governments worldwide understand and communicate their impact on critical sustainability issues such as climate change, human rights, governance and social well-being. This enables real action to create social, environmental and economic benefits for everyone. The GRI Sustainability Reporting Standards are developed with true multi-stakeholder contributions and rooted in the public interest."

The latest issue of the Global Sustainability Standards (G4, from 2015), encompasses 58 general and 92 specific standard disclosures, of which 16 deal directly with labor practices and decent work, and 12 with Human Rights aspects which are especially important in the framework of Sustainable HRM, and show that these guidelines refer to HRM related aspects and thus define what is Sustainable HRM and what not.

In particular, the category Labor Practices and Decent Work, has been predominantly elaborated on the basis of United Nations Conventions and Declarations as well as International Labor Organization Conventions, which shows that the guidelines in this subcategory are linked with the disclosure of demographic aspects, and compliance with minimum standards that define how organizations protect employee rights, foster equality and generate jobs.

With regard to sustainability practices improving the ratio of male to female employees, has become a crucial factor. On the one side, it is an opportunity to help the longevity of the organization and, on the other, a challenge for enterprises to build a group of female workers and a corporate philosophy that supports the development of women.

In addition, the Office of Human Resources Management must ensure that local employment laws are respected with respect to collective agreements, that a trade union-friendly policy is applied, and that employees are included in decision-making procedures.

Moreover, since the working environment (management culture) influences various work-related issues, health protection and occupational safety measures should be implemented by HRM, in order to guarantee the well-being of the employees. Apart from that, ensuring career development through training courses and programs for individual employees becomes a key task for HR personnel.

Although this is not defined as necessary with regard to achieving economic objectives of the organization, it is regarded as an added value for employees and key stakeholders.

In addition, the Office of Human Resources Management must ensure that the staff are aware of the principles and practices of the sustainable enterprise, so that the organization as such can function in a sustainable manner.

4.2. The Heart of the Matter.

It has been demonstrated that SHRM's main purpose is to bring an organization's business strategy in line with its human resource approach to reach its objectives and, in this context, the focus is on the resource-based company vision as a way to describe how HRM personnel and processes can support sustained competitiveness. As Wright and McMahan have postulated:

> *"The resource-based view of competitive advantage differs from the traditional strategy paradigm in that the emphasis of the resource-based view of competitive advantage is on the link between strategy and the internal resources of the firm."*

Here, it becomes apparent that strategic efforts are mostly linked to financial performance and organizational efficiency. We must bear in mind that the SGRH grew in a dynamic and turbulent environment, in which employers' groups such as trade unions were faced with challenges and the way of working, changed with the implementation of various working time schemes.

In this respect, the globalization also played an important role, concerning the stimulation of the competition amongst companies, with the result that concerns on building shareholder value were growing.

Proponents of SHRM believe that HRM practices are capable of generating this value, and people are the key to bringing results to the business. This accentuation on the interrelationship between HRM and financial, as well as organizational performance is the gist of the matter in SHRM, but not of Sustainable HRM.

It is put forward, that the central feature which distinguishes Sustainable HRM from SHRM, is the demand for more attention on the employee-level outcomes, such as for instance employee well-being, instead of solely focusing on HRM impacts on organizational performance.

In a research carried out by Järlström, Saru and Vanhala (2018) from a large number of Finnish public and private enterprises from different business backgrounds, senior managers of these enterprises were asked how they understood the concept of sustainable human resource management, and how they identified and prioritised relevant parties in this context. The research showed four types of sustainable human resource management: fairness and equality, transparency of human resources, cost-effectiveness of employee welfare and that can also be linked to four broader areas of responsibility: - legal and ethical, management, social and economic.

Interestingly enough, the ecological dimension of sustainability was mostly ignored in the top managers' answers. However, their ideas of sustainability and HRM contribute to new key findings in the realm of Sustainable HRM.

In the next paragraphs, the four main categories and their connection to Sustainable HRM, are going to be outlined in order to generate an awareness for the significance of stakeholders (in this case top managers), with regard to the implementation of Sustainable HRM.

Justice and equality have been identified as a dimension in Sustainable HRM, regarding the responsible and sustainable execution of HRM. Although adhering to laws and regulations does not mean that an organization is sustainable, it may be assumed that no benefit is gained in HRM by just obeying the law. In fact, in order to acquire a benefit, the companies need to go beyond these requirements, as the following quote shows:

"Sustainable HRM includes all issues related to the employment relationship and further linked to the collective agreements and laws. In the same vein, the proper management of employment relationships is a signal of the responsibility the company has to its employees."

Apart from that, as for diversity management, the significance and acknowledgement of having diversity among the workforce, and the fact they are treated equally was emphasized. Thus, fair treatment serves as the premise upon which the interpretation and elucidation of Sustainable HRM can be founded.

The category of clear HR practice,s relates to a set of HR practices that are normally managed in organisations (hiring and allocation of resources, skills development, incentives, career planning, participation, flexibility), and that are related to HR practices, that have already been described by Ehnert in his Sustainable Human Resource Management model.

In relation to recruitment and resource allocation, senior executives in Finnish companies refer to the importance of having the right person in the right position at the right time, including in their argumentation a long-term perspective that also reflects a typical feature of sustainable human resource management.

Competence development was regarded as a sign that the company cared about its employees, and was linked to the organization's viability. The top management also understands that although competence development rather aims at profitability and success of the firm, it is the company that is responsible for their employees, especially concerning the employability (within or outside the organization) of the individuals.

Thus, even tough, managers highlighted the win-win situation of competence development for both sides, they also stressed the significance of economic responsibility apart from their managerial responsibility.

The aspect of rewarding was also evaluated as an important feature in the employer-employee relationship and managers underlined the relevance of a transparent rewarding system.

With regard to career planning, which is closely linked to competence development, managers asserted that this can be seen a central feature of Sustainable HRM, since career planning represents a way to find qualified and valuable employees who are devoted to the company.

Also, here a win-win situation for both sides is being established. In this context, employee participation plays another important role with respect to Sustainable HRM. Managers noticed the significance of participation in the form of a two-way communication and the fact that participation can help foster an open communication culture of an organization, which is an integral part of Sustainable HRM.

Furthermore, flexibility was associated with sustainability in HRM, too. Being flexible with regard to employee needs was regarded as an important matter by the managers. In light of this, the management acknowledged the call for individual work approaches, like flexible working hours, leave, remote work, etc, to support employees in striking a balance between work and privacy, as most managers are convinced that these matters will play an essential role in building a sustained long-term competitive advantage. To sum it up, it can be determined that transparent HR practices put in relation to managerial responsibility of Sustainable HRM.

The issue of cost-efficiency in the sustainable management of human resources, is linked to the efficacy of the organization, and covers issues related to the inclusion of human resources management and strategy, proactivity in actions, long-term thinking and business skills of human resources executives. Particularly, long-term thinking is a key feature of Sustainable HRM.

In the study, Finnish senior managers highlighted the relationship between human resource management and the company's strategic objectives. They proposed the idea that the Office of Human Resources Management should support the strategy, and that the issues of the Office of Human Resources Management should be integrated into the strategic debate from the outset.

This strategy-related thinking adds a long-term view to the sustainability discussion, and raises the issue of competitive advantage for the organization. He succeeds in highlighting the call for holistic thinking in Sustainable Human Resources Management, which is related to the vision, strategy, economic resources and environment of the organization.

The task of HRM is to consider the company as an entity as a whole and not only partly. Sustainable HRM then is capable of grasping the value of employees which might in the long run lead to innovation, durability, flexibility and an environment that elevates performance related activities.

The last topic that has been revealed in the study, aims at the employee well-being dimension of Sustainable HRM. This dimension deals with subjects associated with leadership style, as well as taking care and fostering employees.

The emphasis on the well-being aspect, is derived from the criticism that employees are often times regarded as resources that can be consumed like any other resource, disregarding the fact that human resources have special needs and, therefore, need to be treated differently, in the sense that they need to be developed and supported.

Under the umbrella of employee well-being different matters, like physical and mental health, safeguarding the work relationships with supervisors and colleagues, work-life balance, etc. are subsumed. In this context, the managers linked the leadership skills and the ability of taking care of employees, and it was shown that the topic of employee well-being, also stresses the role of well-being in supporting the organization's performance and the mutual gains component.

Consequently, the idea of mutual gains puts forward an optimistic view of the role that employee well-being plays in the HRM and performance relationship. It is believed that HRM has a positive impact on employee well-being as well as organizational performance. Thus, in order to be sustainable, HRM needs to enforce practices that promote – apart from other aspects – the mental and physical health.

As mentioned before the more detailed outline of the study, the employee centered view, or the focus on employee well-being is assumed to be the central difference when comparing SHRM and Sustainable HRM. Due to the fact that the top managers of a numerous amount of Finnish organizations linked employee well-being to sustainability shows how crucial the employee well-being is when talking about Sustainable HRM. Accordingly, the commitment of the managers is regarded as a key to realize sustainability.

Overall, the findings on the dimension of Sustainable HRM merge managerial, economic, social, legal and ethical facets of sustainability into a single entity. As has been noted already, ecological aspects are for the most part neglected and, thus, strengthen Ehnert's model of Sustainable HRM. Although ecological aspects are crucial in organizations, they are also affiliated with sustainable management in general rather than HRM in particular.

However, as studies in the realm of Green HRM have shown, implementing HR practices that are based on Green HRM could lead to better organizational performance and employee well-being provided that environmental management is linked to HRM, too.

4.3. The Connection between Sustainability and SHRM.

In research on sustainability, three key ideas haven been identified to characterize the notion of corporate sustainability: the triple bottom-line model, the integration of short- and long-term effects, and the consumption of income, not capital. Therefore, it is reasonable to take a closer look on these factors and elaborate why it could make sense for the area of HRM to establish Sustainable HRM as an alternative approach.

Hülsmann (2004), has identified links between sustainability and SHRM and addresses three key issues: the integrative analysis of short- and long-term effects and contribution to the longevity of the organization, the consideration of economic, ecological and social aspects simultaneously and, therefore, extension of the strategic goals, and the three different definitions of sustainability, that offer an opportunity for connecting them to Strategic Management. Apart from that, the idea of strategy and sustainability can be linked with regard to the selection of goals and instruments to acquire them. At this point, Hülsmann concludes that concerning the research questions both areas, show some overlapping which is the reason why they can contribute to each other.

In her dissertation, Ehnert then deduced intersections that allow to better understand the link between sustainability and SHRM.

She explains that the following aspects might especially be helpful with regard to solving the problem of labor shortage, and side and feedback effects: first, the concept of the capability to sustain the HR base from within by developing and controlling self-induced, side and feedback effects on the human resource base and the origin of human resources (the source of resources);

second, the idea of extending the concept of strategic success in HRM from a substance-oriented rationality and by contrasting it with existing rationalities;

and third, the idea of maintaining the longevity of an organization by considering short- and long-terms impacts on the HR base.

As these above-mentioned aspects are considered to be crucial for further theorizing on sustainability and SHRM, the following paragraphs will focus on these points, and their shortcomings in SHRM from a sustainability perspective.

The first contribution of sustainability to SHRM is the matter of maintaining resources, also referred to as the concept of utilizing income not capital. The resource-oriented definition of sustainability relates to the understanding rooted in the sustainability concept to the capability of HRM, to foster and perpetuate the HR base of an organization from inside, while simultaneously making sure that human resources are deployed in an efficient and effective manner.

Included to this understanding of professional deployment and regeneration, is the investment into relevant structures and processes, in order to have qualified personnel available in the forthcoming periods. However, the efficient assignment of personnel is not considered to be enough for the longevity of an organization.

Therefore, the relationship between HRM and critical corporate surroundings plays an important role, based on the fact that the longevity of a company and long-lasting availability of human resources is also determined by the viability of the "source of resources".

Consequently, to maintain the HR base from within, it is necessary that HRM is expanded to look after the relationships to the sources of human resources, like families, labor markets, education systems, etc.

In SHRM, one of the key questions is how a company is capable of building and renewing strategic human and organizational resources, in order to generate competitive advantage. In this context, the RBV of the firm has tried to offer plausible answers to this question. With regard to Sustainable HRM, the central difference in answering this question can be found in the presumption about the origin of human resources and the relationship between HRM and the organizational surroundings.

In SHRM literature, the origin of human resources is described as "pool of skills", and the labor markets as "pool of resources", which then turn out to be challenging when these resources are rare.

Yet, from an RBV perspective, rare human resources do not automatically raise a problem, because they can still contribute to developing sustained competitive advantage. However, it is assumed that, not only labor becomes short, but also the capability of the origin of human resources to recreate and provide new resources.

In this context, according to the RBV, human resources as such are not valuable, they only become valuable if they can be utilized for producing for the markets. At this point, it should be noted that in Strategic Management literature, labor shortage is generally regarded as a failure of the markets. This means that dealing with labor shortage focuses on the improvement of crucial HR activities, such as recruitment and retention methods which need to be exploited to their full potential.

Still, managing these shortages, is considered to be unsatisfactory in the realm of sustainability. Therefore, from a sustainability viewpoint, this calls for a more thoughtful approach to HRM, and for controlling internalities and externalities of HR activities on the employees, the current and future HR base. However, as the future HR base cannot be grasped notionally, the focus of attention shifts to the sources of resources.

Considering the extension of the concept of strategic success, it has to be noted that two perceptions of sustainability can be identified: sustainability as a value (i.e. social responsibility), or sustainability as a rationale to cope with human resources.

The economic line of argumentation for sustainability can be either efficiency- and innovation-, or substance-oriented. Under efficiency- and innovation-oriented reasoning all actions that pursue the maximization of the input-output ratio of corporate resources are subsumed, while substance-oriented reasoning deals with actions that seek to balance corporate resource consumption and resource reproduction in the long run.

In the HRM context, the efficiency orientation towards sustainability implies establishing HR activities which lead to deploy employees more efficiently, or to use innovations for assigning less people for the same amount of work. The main goal here is a better financial performance and sustainability, is understood in the sense of an instrument that supports achieving this goal. With regard to the substance orientation, the essential intention of HRM is to maintain the employees' capability to accomplish their tasks and to uphold the source of resources to guarantee the supply of qualified people.

Accordingly, it can be summarized that there are two reasons for the reasoning of sustainability from a social responsibility frame of reference: first, it is discussed that organizations have to reduce externalities on their employees since this is considered to be (socially) responsible behavior and this again is ethical and preferable; second, the reason is more instrumental because it has turned out that social legitimacy came to be a crucial goal for SHRM.

Following this reasoning, it can be said that outlining sustainability as a value, only ignores the fact that sustainability can also be economically rational, but outlining sustainability as a rationale only ignores the fact that some stakeholders await managers to act socially responsible.

Thus, if sustainability is considered from a social responsibility, the explanation behind it can still be economically rational, which it is in the sense of an instrumental value.

In the SHRM literature, the identity of the HRM role is intensely influenced by the call for contribution to corporate performance. The roles of HRM in the various approaches of SHRM have been outlined in chapter 2 of this book.

However, it should be remarked here, that some writers in the realm of SHRM are quite critical towards the role of HRM, and have recognized possibly harmful effects of HRM. The reasons for this can be traced back to the fact that HR executives and researchers want to legitimize their own professions and support HR personnel, in them, at times weaker positions compared to other management functions, like finance and marketing.

In considering HRM as a positive function in itself, one runs into danger of neglecting self-induced feedback effects of HR practices and strategies on organizations themselves on future HRM situations. By integrating the notion of sustainability, the boundaries of HRM are shifted and the source of resources as well as a reciprocal relationship between HRM, and these sources are included and consequently, a broader understanding of strategic success is established.

The last aspect in this context, the consideration of short- and long-term effects is one of the key concepts for sustainability. This key element is described as the idea to consume income not capital. For HRM, the main goal is to have human resources at its disposal now and in the future, which can be traced back to the idea of balancing consumption and reproduction of resources of a company over a long-lasting calendar time.

For the sustainability approach, the temporal dimension, which consists of the long-term actions of success and the deliberation of time as a variable in HRM theories, turns out to be more and more significant. With regard to the ecological dimension of sustainability, the temporal factor has been reviewed multiple times.

The main issue in the context of this debate, is the concern that the regeneration of natural resources is unable to uphold the speed of resource consumption, which seems to be quite careless. The regeneration of human resources is a timely undertaking, and this time is often not taken into account. Then, it is possible that employers consider these times as wasted time as discussions about the justification of HR advancement, and training show if it cannot be proved that these measures contribute to organizational performance.

Thus, the temporal dimension is of relevance from a sustainability viewpoint because HR internalities and economic impacts emerge over time.

It has been proposed that sustainability research comprises the idea of merging the future and the present for SHRM. Further, it has been asserted that organizational change and restructuring processes are speeding up more and more, as a result of innovations and new technical developments and thus, time advanced to a significant conception.

The relevance of the time dimension is revealed when considering the time frame of decision-making and the time cycle for human resources. The decision-making process in SHRM is long-term oriented, and its consequences with regard to individual well-being, organizational effectiveness and community well-being, have been described in classical HRM models.

However, back in the 1980's, when these models were elaborated, the understanding of time was a different one to today's perception of time. Back then, the long-term time horizon was interpreted as a 10-to 20-year time frame, and the answer to the challenge of having human resources available was HR planning. Today, in a more complex and dynamic environment, HR planning has come to its limitations.

In the SHRM literature, it is also mentioned that short-and long-term objectives need to be balanced, and it is noticed that this is a recurring topic in the field of SHRM, for instance as the idea of short-term responsiveness and long-term agility. Also, the theme of time cycles recurs in HRM.

The challenge for HRM here is to explain why their outcomes take a longer time than other management functions in the organization. For HR executives keeping up with changes in their environment is almost impossible, because people cycles take a longer time than financial capital market cycles. As change is speeding up and time becomes scarce, Ehnert suggest to think about the underlying conceptualization of time in the realm of SHRM. In her research, as no similar publications could be found, she draws upon the key findings by Mosakowski and Earley (2000) who have identified future-oriented perceptions which they interpret as the researcher's

"shared interest in the usefulness of strategy ideas for managerial behaviors in the future"

and can be considered as a commonality between SHRM and the sustainability discussion.

Furthermore, it has to be remarked that, although researchers are concerned with the longevity of an organization, the time dimension has mostly been ignored as a variable in the different theories of HRM. Few models include the concept of time; however, it is often only explored indirectly. In this context, it has been purported that certain historical conditions allow organizations to generate a sustained competitive advantage, because it can benefit from being the first in the business sector, the so-called first mover advantage. This means that a company can generate a competitive advantage on the attainment and advancement of resources in earlier time periods, as Barney (2002) has stated:

"In these earlier periods, it is often not clear what the full future value of particular resources will be. Because of this uncertainty, firms are able to acquire or develop these resources for less than what will turn out to be their full value. However, once the full value of these resources is revealed, other firms seeking to acquire or develop these resources will need to pay their full known value, which (in general) will be greater than the costs incurred by the firm that acquired or developed these resources in some earlier period."

This factor is also valid with regard to implementing Sustainable HRM.

4.4. From Strategic HRM to Sustainable HRM: a new approach?

The rising interest in researching on the relationship between sustainability and HRM, can be attributed to a period where the race about hiring the best and most qualified employees becomes increasingly critical for most of the global organizations, where the rational planning approach of SHRM appears to have reached its limits, and where HRM executives are confronted with ambiguous decision-making options, inconsistent requests and strategic tensions.

It is assumed that there are several different factors that go along with the pursuit of integrating sustainability into HRM practice and theory and, thus, the sustainability debate can be considered as the latest trend in the realm of people management. One of the indicators is the fact that the general academic interest regarding the sustainability theme appears to be increasing lately. This has been shown by Jones-Christensen et al. (2007), who conducted a study where they reviewed the curricula of 50 global business schools worldwide.

They revealed that topics like sustainability and Corporate Social Responsibility, have been implemented into the syllabus only a little time after the debate on sustainability was launched with the Brundtland Report. Nowadays, almost half of the reviewed business schools have centers or institutes that deal with the topic of sustainability. Apart from that, in the HRM field writers have started using the notion of sustainability in a context other than sustained competitive advantage. It has been observed that ethical reflections with regard to the stakeholders have gained in importance as especially non-governmental organizations, started calling attention to economic, ecological and social aspects.

Also, besides developments in the relationships of businesses and their environments as well as corporate misconduct, the literature in the realm of sustainability refers to other trends that can be put into the context of the significance of sustainability for HRM. These are, for instance, and without any claim of completeness: intensive work, internationalization and globalization and diversity, demographic trends, labor market developments, the lack of quality in some educational systems and changes regarding the employment relationships and its impacts on the psychological contract.

For a deeper understanding of the emergence of sustainability in the field of people management, in the following paragraphs attention is drawn to demographic developments, tight labor markets and changes in the employment relationship.

With regard to demographic trends and aging workforces, it is assumed that, for several industrialized countries, a labor shortage can be expected.

As birth rates are not sufficient to reproduce the population in many countries, as companies prefer younger employees over older ones, and as more and more older employees chose to retire earlier because they want to prevent negative impacts from working, it will be challenging for organizations to hire the appropriate employees.

Therefore, although corporate HRM is not yet influenced by demographic developments, it is suggested to invest in a proactive and sustainable HRM in order to avoid negative outcomes. In this context, the aspect of tight labor markets plays another significant role, as they represent important corporate surroundings making pools of potential future employees available.

For HRM research, providing qualified and motivated people to organizations is of central interest. However, regardless of globalization, labor markets are most of the time nationally affected because of legislative and regulatory stipulations.

The central reasons for tight labor markets are that less young people enter the labor market due to decreasing birth rates, while older workers tend to retire earlier. On top of that, a lot of job candidates do often not have the right or desired qualification, with the consequence of high unemployment rates and labor shortage at the same time.

On the other hand, those who are highly qualified and bring a long, the requested competencies are often able to choose between different job offers. Since worldwide the request for qualified personnel exceeds the existing supply, and as the same organizations have access to the same pool of talents, the expectations of employees have changed, particularly concerning the benefits other than financial aspects offered by the employers.

Another moving force in the whole sustainability, debate can be found in the employment relationship. What meant here is the relationship between employer and employee, which is no longer described as a long-term or even life-long relationship, but rather as a contract based economic exchange.

While back in the day employees often started working for an organization as an apprentice, and then stayed with the company for their entire working life, the situation nowadays has changed.

In these fast-living times with competitive pressure of modern business life, a lot of organizations have noted that they cannot guarantee the jobs of their employees, like it was the case in the past and that they had to release part of their workforce in order to remain competitive and become more flexible.

As a consequence, employees began to show more initiative regarding the development of their careers and their employability, and their loyalty towards their employer has been scrutinized. This has been purported by Tsui and Wu (2005), to be one of the reasons why the new employment relationship is economically not as appealing as its proponents propose. They believe that the reciprocal investment employment relationship, is more encouraging with regard to performance.

In this context, the topic of "psychological contracts" has gained significance, and contributes to the understanding of the mutual exchange processes between employee and employer. This matter has been treated by Rousseau (1995), who defined those contracts as the individuals' beliefs about terms and conditions about this exchange relationship, and revealed that these obligations and promises are for the most part not fixed in employment contracts, as they are not written down and sometimes even not even mentioned presumptions.

Consequently, these expectations might differ depending on the perspective. In this regard, understanding the psychological contract and the underlying processes is one of the key concerns for recruiting and retaining employees.

It is assumed that the above-mentioned issues, have an impact on the HR base and the future availability of qualified and talented employees. The outlined developments suggest that the shift towards a resource orientation of HRM, might be extended towards an interest in and an understanding for sustainability.

The question that remains to be answered now, is whether or not the approach of Sustainable HRM represents a new concept of managing people.

The so far discussed aspects in the context of sustainability and HRM, show that there is potential for an alternative way of conceptualizing HRM and the outcomes of people management. Even though there is no coherent body of literature on Sustainable HRM, the three identified streams in the field of Sustainable HRM all focus on the development of human resources as a vital outcome of HRM processes, and the primary purpose of HRM, which is described as the achievement of business, outcomes in SHRM literature is queried.

Additionally, the longevity of the organization and the HRM processes and outcomes that play an important part in the survival of the company, are of utmost interest in research activities on this topic. Even in the literature on Green HRM, the interdependencies between social and ecological outcomes, and organizational sustainability and business performance is recognized. As has been shown, the literature on Sustainable HRM stresses a couple of aspects that differentiate Sustainable HRM from SHRM, and, therefore, offers the possibility for further advancement.

It also has been asserted that Sustainable HRM does not exclude features of SHRM or personnel management. Just like SHRM integrates aspects of personnel management, Sustainable HRM includes aspects of the afore mentioned approaches. But, in order to represent a totally new approach to people management, it would need a considerably different orientation towards SHRM.

Moreover, some of the aspects mentioned in the Sustainable HRM literature, encompass theoretical, moral, practice, outcomes and process issues which are considered to be interdependent. However, what links all these issues, is a clear focus on the objective of HRM practices.

In SHRM, the focal point is advancing organizational performance, particularly with regard to economic outcomes.

In Sustainable HRM, to focus is broader and it's all about advancing not only economic outcomes by means ends, but also a variety of outcomes, namely social and ecological ones. This center of attraction acknowledges the cross-linking of many features of the organization, the people within, and the surroundings.

In the literature on Sustainable HRM, theoretical aspects affiliated with HRM features, can be found which incorporate the dynamic nature of HRM and its outcomes, the interrelation of internal, external and individual people aspects of organizations, and the need to take into account the outcomes with regard to not only organizational economic outcomes, but also economic, ecological and social outcomes for the different stakeholders.

Furthermore, issues which center around the capabilities, the complexity and the ambiguities linked with the execution and implementation of HRM and the role of HR executives, are raised concerning the HRM practice. These capabilities are considered to be essential for successful management now and in the future, and especially in a progressively sensitive ecological environment.

Writers on Sustainable HRM also emphasize some essential characteristics of organizational outcomes, which question the SHRM perspective. Human outcomes, either with regard to being beneficial for the longevity of the company or as a means ends, represent a coherent topic in the literature.

Additionally, in some documents, the significance of HRM practices regarding ecological outcomes is highlighted. Apart from that, the identification and assessment of negative outcomes would be an essential feature of Sustainable HRM.

To conclude, it can be noted that Sustainable HRM represents an alternative approach to managing people.

However, in the sense of an extension to personnel management and SHRM. In the literature, a couple of implications of a Sustainable HRM approach for research and HRM practice, can be found and the significance of recognizing the impact of HRM on other than economic outcomes has been acknowledged, although the writings in the field do not consist of a coherent body of literature. Sustainable HRM queries the:

"existing focus of HRM contributing to only financial outcomes, the role of the HR professional as a business partner and the role of human and social outcomes of HRM merely in terms of their contribution to business outcomes. It raises the importance of making explicit the moral dimensions of HRM policy, the interests that are served by policy and the interconnectedness of internal and external outcomes resulting form these policies. A critical aspect of these requirements is the explicit statement of the assumptions which underpin the purpose of HRM."

Therefore, Sustainable HRM can be considered as a new approach of people management, by recognizing further intentions for HRM with regard to the identification of complex workplace dynamics, and the necessity to prevent negative impacts of HRM practices. However, it is indispensable to acknowledge the fact that, features of personnel management and SHRM, also represent an integral part of Sustainable HRM. On that account, organizational outcomes and economic key figures also belong to Sustainable HRM.

5. Case Study: The Bremer Landesbank and Sustainable HRM.

After having outlined the theoretical framework of SHRM and in particular Sustainable HRM, attention is now drawn to the practical application of Sustainable HRM. As an example of what Sustainable HRM can contribute to development and longevity of the organization, the case of the Bremer Landesbank will be examined more closely.

The Bremer Landesbank has decided to implement a Sustainable HRM, with the consequence that initiatives of personnel risk management and capability-oriented succession planning have become more important. As banks are knowledge-intensive service companies, the long-term competitive position does not merely depend on their returns, but on the impact of their investments in human resources.

Products of credit institutes are highly homogenous, in need of explanation and imitable. However, this does not apply for the quality of the personally performed service, which is generally rooted in the qualification and competency, the motivation and commitment of the employees.

These factors represent the decisive competitive advantage in this branch. Therefore, the Bremer Landesbank, has decided to turn its attention to a sustainability perspective with regard to HRM. According to what has been outlined before, concerning Sustainable HRM, the Bremer Landesbank subsumes two significant directions: first, maintaining the HR base and, second, replenishing i.e. ensuring enough supply for the HR base.

Points of reference are the necessary human resources and specific personnel management activities, like personnel evaluation, compensation, and development. In this context, the Bremer Landesbank includes a distinct and above average social responsibility for employees and other stakeholders into its understanding of Sustainable HRM.

With regard to maintaining the HR base, measures that assure the personnel structure performance consist of measures that maintain and enhance the motivation and the commitment of the employees, actively and positively support change management aspects, adapt competencies and qualifications to future needs, retain high performers, and serve the employees with regard to physical and mental resilience in order to maintain the level of performance.

Replenishment of the HR base is understood as personnel supplement for the workforce from either internal potential, but also external sources. The Bremer Landesbank states that strategic HR planning and HR controlling, as well as understanding of leadership and leadership culture are to be regarded as an explicit and implicit body of control and management.

However, new to the concept of Sustainable HRM are not the different instruments and measures of personnel management, but rather the structure and the prioritization. They do not follow a functional or procedural structure, but the strategic incentive to maintain and replenish the HR base on a long-term basis. That is the reason, why for Sustainable HRM it can be purported: structure follows sustainability. In this context, the discussion about the HR business partner model is put to the background, while necessary initiatives of HR risk management and succession planning gain in importance.

In the sense of maintaining and replenishing the HR base, the Bremer Landesbank has focused its HR activities on structured identification of HR risks and succession planning, which means that HR risks are to be intercepted proactively and on a long-term basis through identification and promotion of high potentials.

This is accomplished through the following measures, that are conducted on an annual basis: identification and evaluation of HR risks, analytical consideration of risk situations, bank-wide identification of high potentials for the successions or deputies, deduction of fields of action for leadership personnel and HR initiatives.

Here, central to success is the participation and involvement of the board of directors and management executives, because that is how a common awareness for the urgency of sustainability in the realm of HR, could be underlined. Of utmost importance in this context, is the plausibility of standardization of high-potential employees, or to be more precise the specific potential statement where the sustainability claim has to be taken seriously, because the HR base will be endangered if the replenishment decisions are made due to irregular assessments.

For this reason, the Bremer Landesbank does not only rely on assessment centers, but uses other diagnostics, such as interviews, simulations of different tasks and scientific questionnaires that deal with the suitability and motivation of the job candidates to find the appropriate employees.

Thus, breaking it down, Sustainable HRM as executed by the Bremer Landesbank, means running a qualitative and quantitative monitoring of the staff, with regard to risk and potential aspects, identifying and fostering high-potentials, mitigating HR risks and focusing on maximum quality concerning the processes, methods and systems of recruiting and retaining employees, in particular in order not to endanger or harm the sustainability aspects in the whole process.

Another aspect that has been brought up in the sustainability debate in the Bremer Landesbank, is the topic of dialogue with the employees through employee surveys.

It is obvious that Sustainable HRM does not work without a sophisticated understanding for the specific needs of the employees. HR personnel, who are not able to evaluate the performance and motivation of the workforce, cannot implement a Sustainable HRM.

Thus, it has been shown that a structured dialogue with the employees appears to be very promising with regard to implement, and realize Sustainable HRM. The feedback of the employees enables HR executives to identify main parameters and levers to systematically, deal with strengths and weaknesses in this field.

However, it is important to know that, since the effort behind such surveys is enormous employee, surveys not only need to be conducted, but their results need to be evaluated correctly and the right conclusions need to be drawn.

The consequence from this instrument is that the execution of surveys such be well-considered, because if taken seriously, month-long or even longstanding processes are going to take place in the aftermath. However, there will be an effect that cannot be realized otherwise: employee surveys represent the key aspect with regard to communication and information for HR management in Sustainable HRM.

Thus, HR executives strongly depend on a structured dialogue (preferably through surveys) with the employees of the company in order to maintain and replenish the HR base.

On that account, all of the above shows that Sustainable HRM remains an empty phrase without precise profiling of the HR work. This concerns quite a couple of the personnel initiative, for instance, target-group-specific implementation of health and social counseling, the regional enforcement of employer attractivity, reconcilability of family and working life, to just mention a few.

Thus, factors that are critical to success concerning the implementation of Sustainable HRM are to be found in the company management, the organizational structure and the strategy development, since the conceptualization and implementation of a Sustainable HRM represents a shift of paradigm for the organization.

6. Conclusion & Discussion.

The present book has dealt with SHRM, Sustainable HRM and the differences and commonalities of the two of them. The main objective was to show where both approaches can be distinguished from each other, and where similarities can be found.

In the first part of the book, the intention was to create a common basis of understanding of the SHRM approach, by offering definitions for the term strategy and human resources. Concerning the notion of strategy, it has been shown that it can be understood as a link of manifold individual decisions, with the aim of generating a harmonization or strategic match between the institution and its environment.

Further, Mintzberg et al. (2003), who offer five different interpretations of strategy, have distinguished between intended and realized strategies, and purported that realized strategies are not always intended, but they can be located between deliberate and emergent strategies. This understanding of strategy acknowledges the fact that strategy, has different perspectives in corporate practice, und integrates the perception that realized strategies cannot be planned rationally and comprehensively beforehand.

With regard to human resources, it has been outlined that human resources are more than just a resource, that is traded on the market like the other resources, and that humans, have special needs that need to be taken care of. Therefore, Barney's definition of human capital where human resources are described as:

"the training, experience, judgement, intelligence, relationships, and insight of individual managers and workers in a firm"

and Jackson and Schuler's (2006) definition that human resources are not only the current employees, but also those who one day might be working for the organization seem to be plausible.

Regarding the definition of SHRM, it has been shown that an integrative definition which considers an understanding and affecting relationship, is the most promising in this context.

Thereafter, the most popular theoretical frameworks of SHRM, were introduced and outlined with main focus on the resource-based view of the firm. Regarding best practice and best fit, both may be right in their own way, as the whole debate actually represents two sides of the same coin, and both are relevant in exploring the linkage between HRM and performance.

It has been indicated that the RBV differs from the traditional strategy paradigm in that the accentuation, is on the link between strategy and the internal resources of the firm. As has been stated by Jiang et al. (2013):

"A key essence of this perspective is that internal assets of organizations, such as human capital, have the potential to prove value in setting firms apart from their competitors and have the potential to serve as a barrier to imitation if managed appropriately."

The second part of the paper focused on the concept of Sustainable HRM. Similar to the first part, definitions on sustainability and Sustainable Resource Management were presented to establish a basis for the explanation of the approach of Sustainable HRM.

In this context, the report of the Brundtland Commission and the evolvement of the triple-bottom-line model, have been mentioned and different definitions on Sustainable HRM haven been offered. In the subchapter on different approaches in Sustainable HRM, it has been shown that three different groups have been identified that deal with the notion of sustainability in HRM.

However, as the research in this field is still at an early stage, an operationalization has not taken place yet and only few models on Sustainable HRM exist. However, Ehnert can be considered to be conceptionally relevant, as her research and work contributed to a large extent to the development and dissemination of this topic in the international research community. Also, her definition of Sustainable HRM, has been widely accepted amongst international researchers and used as a basis to be further enhanced.

In the third part, the main goal was to contrast the SHRM approach with the concept of Sustainable HRM, in order to expose the differences and commonalities between the two concepts, and apart from that, to answer the question whether or not Sustainable HRM represents a shift of paradigm and a new approach.

It has been demonstrated that in Sustainable HRM, a shift of paradigm can be observed since new features, such as the consideration of more than just financial outcomes, the consideration of more stakeholders, and the fact that, HR measures outside of the organization need to be taken into account, have been adopted.

Regarding the central difference between SHRM and Sustainable HRM, a study by Jarlström, Saru and Vanhala (2018), has been introduced that perfectly illustrates the fact that the well-being of the employee gains in importance, and is to be considered as the most important difference between the two concepts of people management.

However, it also has been demonstrated that there are parallels and commonalities both concepts share. The main take-away of this comparison though is that the main difference between the two approaches is the employee-centered view in Sustainable HRM, which does not play a decisive role in SHRM.

Apart from that, what is to be considered as important or even more important, is the fact that Sustainable HRM is to be regarded as an extension of SHRM, because Sustainable HRM contains the major aspects of SHRM, but then takes on the next step in the evolution of people management by really focusing on the heart of the matter, or, in other words, the Heart in Human Resource Management: the human beings.

References:

Avery, G., Bergsteiner, H. (2010). Honeybees and Locustus: The Business Case for Sustainable Leadership. St.Leonards: Allen & Unwin.

Baird, L., Meshoulam, I. (1988). Managing two fits of strategic human resource management. Academy of Management Review 13(1), 116-128.

Barney, J. (1991). Firm resources and sustained competitive advantage. Journal of Management 17(1), 99-120.

Barney, J. (2002). Gaining and sustaining competitive advantage, 2nd edn. Prentice Hall, New Jersey.

Boudreau, J.W., Ramstad, P.M. (2005). Talentship, talent segmentation, and sustainability: A new HR decision science paradigm for a new strategy definition. Human Resource Management 44(2), 129-136.

Boxall, P. (1996). The strategic HRM debate and the resource-based view of the firm. Human Resource Management Journal 6(3), 59-75.

Boxall, P. (1998). Achieving competitive advantage through human resource strategy: towards a theory of industry dynamics. Human Resource Management Review 8(3), 265-288.

Boxall, P. (1999). Human resource strategy and industry-based competition: a conceptual framework and agenda for theoretical development. In: Wright, P., Dyer, L., Boudreau, J., Milkovich, G. (eds): Research in Personnel and Human Resource Management (Supplement 4: Strategic Human Resource Management in the Twenty-First Century). JAI Press, Stamford, CT, London, UK.

Boxall, P. (2014). The future of employment relations from the perspective of human resource management. Journal of Industrial Relations, 56(4), 578-593.

Boxall, P., Purcell, J. (2000). Strategic human resource management: where have we come from and where should we be going? International Journal of Management Reviews 2 (2), 183-203.

Boxall, P., Steeneveld, M. (1999). Human resource strategy and competitive advantage: A longitudinal study of engineering consultancies. Journal of Management Studies 36(4), 443-463.

Branco, M., Rodrigues, L. (2006). Corporate Social Responsibility and Resource-Based Perspectives. Journal of Business Ethics 69(2), 111-132.

Brewster, C., Larsen, H. (2000). Human resource management in Europe: trends, dilemmas and strategy. Blackwell, Oxford.

Capelli, P., Singh, H. (1992). Integrating Strategic Human Resources and Strategic Management. In: Lewin, D., Mitchell, O.S., Sherer, P.D. (eds) Research Frontiers in Industrial Relations and Human Resources, Madison, WI: IRRA.

Clarke, M. (ed) (2011). Readings in HRM and sustainability. University Press, Tilde.

Coff, R. (1997). Human assets and management dilemmas: coping with hazards on the road to resource-based theory. Academy of Management Review 22(2), 374-402.

Cohen, E., Taylor, S., Müller-Camen, M. (2012). HRM's role in corporate social and environmental sustainability. SHRM Report.

Collinson, D., Cobb, G., Power, D., Stevenson, L. (2007). The Financial Performance of the FTSE4 Good Indices. Corporate Social Responsibility and Environmental Management 15(1), 14-28.

Docherty, P., Forslin, J., (Rami) Shani, A.B., Kira, M. (eds) (2002). Emerging Work Systems: From Intensive to Sustainable. In Docherty, P., Forslin, J., Shani, A.B. (Rami) (eds) Creating Sustainable Work Systems: Emerging Perspectives and Practice. Routledge, London.

Docherty, P., Kira, M., Shani, A.B. (2009). What the World Needs Now is Sustainable Work Systems. In Docherty, P., Kira, M., Shani, A.B. (eds) Creating Sustainable Work Systems: Developing Social Sustainability (2nd edn). Routledge, London.

Dunford, B.B., Snell, S.A., Wright, P.M. (2001). Human Resources and the Resource Based View of the Firm (CAHRS Working Paper #01-03). Ithaca, NY: Cornell University, School of Industrial and Labor Relations, Center for Advanced Human Resources Studies.

Dunphy, D., Griffiths, A., Benn, S. (2007). Organization Change for Corporate Sustainability (2nd edn). Routledge, London.

Ehnert, I. (2009). Sustainable Human Resource Management. A Conceptual and Exploratory Analysis form a Paradox Perspective, Physica-Verlag, Berlin.

Ehnert, I., Harry, W. (2012). Recent Developments and Future Prospects on Sustainable Human Resource Management: Introduction to the Special Issue. Management Revue 23(3), 221-238.

Friedman, M. (1970). The Social Responsibility of Business is to Increase Profits. New York Times Magazine, September 13, 32-33.

Freitas, W.R., Jabbour, C.J.C., Fernando, C.A.S. (2011). Continuing the evolution: towards sustainable HRM and sustainable organizations. Business Strategy Series 12(5), 226-234.

Gollan, P. (2005). High involvement management and human resource sustainability: The challenges and opportunities. Asia Pacific Journal of Human Resources (43), 18-33.

Guerci, M. (2011). La gestione delle risorse umane per la sostenibilità dell'impresa. Franco Angeli.

Hahn, T., Figge, F. (2011). Beyond the Bounded Instrumentality in Current Corporate Sustainability Research: Toward an Inclusive Notion of Profitability. Journal of Business Ethics (104), 325-345.

Hamel, G., Prahalad C. (1993). Strategy as stretch and leverage. Harvard Business Review 71(2), 75-84.
Hamel, G., Prahalad C. (1994). Competing for the Future. Boston: Harvard Business School Press.
Hoeppe, J.C., Lau, V. (2011). Nachhaltig arbeiten. Personal 5 (2011), 30-33.
Hülsmann, M. (2004). Bezugspunkte zwischen Strategischem Management und Nachhaltigkeit. In: Hülsmann, M., Müller-Christ, G., Haasis, H.-D. (eds) Betriebswirtschaftslehre und Nachhaltigkeit. Deutscher Universitäts-Verlag, Wiesbaden.
Huselid, M.A. (1995). The Impact of Human Resource Management Practices on Turnover, Productivity, and Corporate Financial Performance. Academy of Management Journal 38(3), 635-672.
Jackson, S., Renwick, D., Jabbour, C.J.C., Müller-Camen, M. (2011). State-of-the-Art and Future Directions for Green Human Resource Management: Introduction to the Special Issue. German Journal of Human Resource Management 25(2), 99-116.
Jarlström, M., Saru, E., Vanhala, S. (2018). Sustainable Human Resource Management with Salience of Stakeholders: A Top Management Perspective. Journal of Business Ethics 152, 703-724.
Jiang, K., Takeuchi, R., Lepak, D.P. (2013). Where do We Go From Here? New Perspectives on the Black Box in Strategic Human Resource Management Research. Journal of Management Studies 50(8), 1448-1480.
Jones-Christensen, L., Peirce, E., Hartmann, L.P., Hoffman, W.M., Carrier, J. (2007). Ethics, CSR, and sustainability education in the Financial Times top 50 global business schools: baseline data and future research directions. Journal of Business Ethics 73, 347-368.
Kamoche, K. (1996). Strategic human resource management within a resource-capability view of the firm. Journal of Management Studies 33(2), 213-233.

Kira, M. (2002). Moving From Consuming to Regenerative Work. In Docherty, P., Forslin, J., Shani, A.B. (Rami) (eds) Creating Sustainable Work Systems: Emerging Perspectives and Practice. Routledge, London.

Koch, M.J., McGrath, R.G. (1996). Improving Labor Productivity: Human Resource Management Policies do Matter. Strategic Management Journal (17), 335-354.

Kramar, R. (2012). Human Resources: An Integral Part of Sustainability. In Jones, G. (ed) Current Research in Sustainability, Tilde University Press, Melbourne.

Kramar, R. (2014). Beyond strategic human resource management: is sustainable human resource management the next approach? The International Journal of Human Resource Management 25(8), 1069-1089.

Lado, A.A, Wilson, M.C. (1994). Human Resource Systems and Sustained Competitive Advantage: A Competency-based Perspective. Academy of Management Review 19(4), 699-727.

Lau, V., Moritz, J. (2011). Lob der Nachhaltigkeit. Personalwirtschaft 11/2011, 42-43.

Legge, K. (1978). Power, Innovation and Problem-solving in Personnel Management. London: McGraw-Hill.

Leonard, D. (1992). Core capabilities and core rigidities: a paradox in managing new product development. Strategic Management Journal (13), 111-125.

Leonard, D. (1998). Wellsprings of Knowledge: Building and Sustaining the Sources of Innovation. Boston: Harvard Business School Press.

Lepak, D.P., Snell, S.A. (1999). The human resource architecture: Toward a theory of human capital allocation and development. Academy of Management Review (24), 31-48.

Macharzina, K. (2003). Unternehmensführung: Das internationale Managementwissen, 4th edn. Gabler, Wiesbaden.

Mariappanadar, S. (2003). Sustainable Human Resource Strategy. The Sustainable and Unsustainable Dilemmas of Retrenchment. International Journal of Social Economics 30(8), 906-923.

Mariappanadar, S. (2012). The Harm Indicators of Negative Externality of Efficiency Focused Organisational Practices. International Journal of Social Economics 39, 209-220.

Martin, A. (2003). Personal als Ressource? In: Martin, A. (ed): Personal als Ressource. Rainer Hampp, München, Mering, pp 5-20.

Martín-Alcázar, F., Romero-Fernández, P.M., Sánchez-Gardey, G. (2005). Strategic human resource management: integrating the universalistic, contingent, configurational and contextual perspectives. The International Journal of Human Resource Management, 16(5), 633-659.

Maurer, I., Müller-Camen, M. (2016). Nachhaltiges Personalmanagement. In Doyé, T. (ed) CSR und Human Resource Management, Springer-Verlag, Berlin, Heidelberg.

Miller, D. (1992). Generic strategies; classification, combination and context. Advances in Strategic Management (8), 391-408.

Mintzberg, H., Lampel, J., Quinn, J.B., Goshal, S. (eds) (2003). The strategy process: Concepts, contexts, cases, 4th edn. Pearson Education, New Jersey.

Moldaschl, M., Fischer, D. (2004). Beyond the management view. A resource-centered socio-economic perspective. Management Revue 15(1), 122-152.

Mosakowski, E., Earley, P.C. (2000). A selective review of time assumptions in strategy research. Academy of Management Review 25(4), 796-812.

Mueller, F. (1996). Human resources as strategic assets; an evolutionary resource-based theory. Journal of Management Studies 33(6), 757-785.

Müller-Camen, M., Hartog, M., Morton, C., et al. (2008). Corporate social responsibility and sustainable HRM. In Müller-Camen, M., Croucher, R., Leigh, S. (eds) Human Resource Management: A case study approach. CIPD: London.

Müller-Christ, G. (2001). Nachhaltiges Ressourcenmanagement. Metropolis-Verlag, Marburg.
Müller-Christ, G., Remer, A. (1999). Umweltwirtschaft oder Wirtschaftsökolgie? Vorüberlegungen zu einer Theorie des Ressourcenmanagements. In Seidel, E. (ed) Betriebliches Umweltmanagement im 21. Jahrhundert: Aspekte, Aufgaben, Perspektiven. Springer-Verlag, Berlin.
Ostermann, P. (1994). How common is workplace transformation and who adopts it? Industrial and Labor Relations Review 47(2), 173-188.
Orlitzky, M., Schmidt, F., Rynes, S. (2003). Corporate Social Financial Performance: A Meta-Analysis. Organizational Studies 24(3), 403-441.
Paauwe, J., Boselie, P. (2005). HRM and performance: what next? Human Resource Management Journal 15(4), 68-83.
Pfeffer, J. (1994). Competitive Advantage Through People. Boston: Harvard Business School Press.
Pfeffer, J. (2010). Building sustainable organizations: The human factor. Academy of Management Perspectives 2, 34-45.
Renwick, D.W.S., Redman, T., Maguire, S. (2011). Green Human Resource Management: A Review and Research Agenda. International Journal of Management Reviews 15, 1-14.
Rousseau, D.M. (1995). Psychological contracts in organizations. Understanding written and unwritten agreements. Thousand Oaks, CA: Sage.
Schuler, R.S., Jackson, S.E. (1987). Linking competitive strategies and human resource management practices. Academy of Management Executive 1(3), 207-219.
Schuler, R.S., Jackson, S.E. (2006). Human resource management: international perspectives. Thomson South-West, Mason, OH.
Scholz, C. (1987). Strategisches Management: Ein integrativer Ansatz. Walter de Gruyter, Berlin.

Scholz, C., Müller, S. (2010). Kompetenz4HR: Nachhaltigkeit in der Personalarbeit in Österreich. Saarbrücken: Institut für Managementkompetenz.
Staehle, W.H. (1999). Management: Eine verhaltenswissenschaftliche Perspektive, 8th edn. Vahlen, München.
Tsui, A.J., Wu, J.B. (2005). The new employment relationship versus the mutual investment approach: implications for human resource management. Human Resource Management 44(2), 115-121.
Weinstein, M., Kochan, T. (1995). The limits of diffusion: recent developments in industrial relations and human resource practices in the United States. In: Locke, R., Kochan, T., Piore, M. (eds): Employment Relations in a Changing World Economy. Cambridge, MA: MIT Press.
WCED (1987). Our common future. World Commission on Environment and Development. Oxford University Press, Oxford.
Wilkinson, A., Hill, M. et al. (2001). The sustainability debate. International Journal of Operations & Production Management 21(12), 1492-1502.
Wilkinson, A. (2005). Downsizing, rightsizing or dumbsizing? Quality, Human Resources and the management of sustainability. Total Quality Management 16(8-9), 1079-1088.
Wright, P.M. (1998). Introduction: Strategic Human Resource Management Research in the 21st Century. In: Human Resource Management Review (8), 187-191.
Wright, P.M., McMahan, G.C. (1992). Theoretical Perspectives for Strategic Human Resource Management. Journal of Management, 18(2), 295–320.
Wright, P.M., McMahan, G.C, McWilliams, A. (1994). Human resources and sustained competitive advantage: a resource-based perspective. International Journal of Human Resource Management 5(2), 301-326.

Zaugg, R.J., Blum, A. et al. (2001). Sustainability in Human Resource Management. Working Paper No. 51, Institute for Organization and Personnel. Bern: University of Bern.

Zaugg, R.J., Blum, A., Thom, N. (2001). Sustainability in Human Resource Management: Evaluation Report. IOP-Press, Bern.

Zink, K.J. (2008). Nachhaltigkeitsstrategien und Human Resource Management. In M. von Hauff, V. Lingnau, K.J. Zink (eds) Nachhaltiges Wirtschaften. Nomos: Baden-Baden.

Online resources:

https://www.cornerstoneondemand.de/blog/talent_management/human_resources/hr_history (retrieved 04/22/2019)
https://dictionary.cambridge.org/de/worterbuch/englisch/resource (retrieved 03/18/2019)
https://en.oxforddictionaries.com/definition/resource (retrieved 03/18/2019)
(https://en.wikipedia.org/wiki/Volatility,_uncertainty,_complexity_and_ambiguity/ (retrieved 04/22/2019)
https://www.haufe.de/media/geschichte-des-personalwesens_378692.html (retrieved 04/22/2019)
Kienbaum Management Consultants (2010) Sustainable HR. Zur Rolle der Personalarbeit in einer nachhaltigen Unternehmensführung;
https://imis.de/portal/load/fid813859/Vortrag_MK%C3%B6tter.pdf (retrieved 04/03/2019)
https://www.globalreporting.org/information/about-gri/Pages/default.aspx (retrieved 04/04/2019)
https://www.globalreporting.org/resourcelibrary/GRIG4-Part1-Reporting-Principles-and-Standard-Disclosures.pdf (retrieved 04/04/2019)
https://www.wissen.de/wortherkunft/strategie/ (retrieved 03/06/2019)

www.ingramcontent.com/pod-product-compliance
Lightning Source LLC
Chambersburg PA
CBHW072201170526
45158CB00004BB/1730